The Azusa Street
REVIVAL

The Azusa Street

REVIVAL

WHEN THE FIRE FELL

ROBERTS LIARDON

Destiny Image® Publishers, Inc.
P.O. Box 310
Shippensburg, PA 17257-0310

"Speaking to the Purposes of God for this Generation
and for the Generations to Come."

For Worldwide Distribution, Printed in the U.S.A.

ISBN 10: 0-7684-2366-X
ISBN 13: 978-0-7684-2366-2

This book and all other Destiny Image, Revival Press, MercyPlace, Fresh Bread, Destiny Image Fiction, and Treasure House books are available at Christian bookstores and distributors worldwide.

For a U.S. bookstore nearest you, call
1-800-722-6774.

For more information on foreign distributors, call
717-532-3040.

Or reach us on the Internet:
www.destinyimage.com

4 5 6 7 8 9 10 11 / 14 13 12 11

ISBN 978-0-7684-1319-9

CONTENTS

ACKNOWLEDGMENTS

Special thanks:

To Don Milam for assisting me with the research and writing of this project.

To Glenn Gohr and all the good folk at the Flower Pentecostal Heritage Center for the use of photos from their archive. For more information on Pentecostal history, I suggest you visit their Website at: www.agheritage.org

INTRODUCTION

GIVEN all the demands that press in upon us as we deal with the stress of the present moment and living in angst about what is to come, it is easy to become disconnected from our past. Why even bother with what has been? Yet, as someone has said, if we don't learn from the past, we are doomed to repeat the past. That is the negative side of why we should study the history of the Church. The positive side is that there is much in the past that will inspire, breathe into us hope, and create fresh motivation for our own historical journey. History is the harbor of our heritage and the fountainhead of our families.

History helps us understand our past so that we can better understand who we are. History provides inspiration for the present and hope for the future. The lives of those in the past, along with their courage and their discoveries, give us renewed focus for our own lives. Studying the stories of individuals and situations in the past allows us to test our own moral sense, to hone it against some of the real complexities individuals have faced in difficult settings. The people who have weathered adversity in real-life circumstances provide inspiration.

History gives you back your past. In the same way that individuals need memory to shape identity and plan for the future, communities need history to give dimension and meaning to the present. On the other hand, without an understanding of the past, the present doesn't make much sense.

The study of history gives us a sense of God's purposes in the affairs of men. What He has done for others, He will do for us. He visited people in the past with His presence and power, which gives us hope that He will let His fire fall upon us as well.

The modern Pentecostal movement began in April 1906 in an insignificant little building in Los Angeles at 312 Azusa Street. As we will look at later in this book, there were many other events of spiritual activity that led up to the inauguration of present-day Pentecostalism; but without a doubt, Azusa Street was the watershed moment that led to a tidal wave of revival fervor spreading from Los Angeles to every part of the world.

In the face of external opposition and ridicule, internal bickering and theological differences, the Azusa Street revival marked the beginning of the renewal of the Spirit. The fires of revival at Azusa Street would eventually spread over the next 100 years and into the third wave of Christianity. Starting with the time of Constantine, the Roman Catholic Church became the first wave. Next, when Martin Luther nailed his 95 theses on the door at Wittenburg, the Protestant reformation began and developed as the second wave. Then, at 312 Azusa Street, with an unlikely group of spiritually hungry saints, the beginnings of a tsunami of spiritual power and passion flooded every country of the world. Pentecostalism became the third wave, and it continues to impact nations worldwide. A Pentecostal preacher summed up the history of Pentecostalism by saying, "The Lord took the Baptist water and the Methodist fire and made the Pentecostal steam."

Every revival eventually reaches a certain apex at which time suddenly and dramatically the world is drawn to that place and the course of history is shifted. The progression of truth moved people forward, and as new truth was being revealed, God's people were being directed into new places of spiritual reality.

But no great historical event is birthed in a vacuum, isolated by itself. There have always been certain events, people, and circumstances that prepare the way for the final manifestation that catches the attention of the entire world. This book not only explores the momentous events surrounding the Azusa Street Revival but also examines the events that led up to that memorable event.

WHO ARE THE PENTECOSTALS?

Experience, rather than doctrine, has often been noted as the principal reality and heart of Pentecostalism. Although the Pentecostals are conservative in their theology, they are passionate in their spiritual experiences. The emphasis on the Holy Spirit is essential to Pentecostal reality, and almost all Pentecostal denominations believe that the "initial evidence" of Spirit baptism is the manifestation of glossolalia or what is commonly referred to as "speaking in tongues." Life within the Pentecostal churches is enhanced by manifestations of the gifts of the Spirit, dynamic worship, and evangelistic fervor.

Pentecostal worship is characterized by praying in tongues, prophesying, healings, hand-clapping, and dynamic preaching, which are all enjoyed with great zeal and fervency. This worship style divides Pentecostals from other mainline Christian denominations.

Pentecostals believe in a separate experience known as the baptism of the Spirit. This experience is evidenced by speaking in tongues and a renewed experience of spiritual power in their life. With the coming of the Spirit, God also has given them access to the other gifts of the Spirit: the ability to prophesy, divine healing, words of wisdom, words of knowledge, the discernment of spirits, etc.

But the Pentecostal beliefs are more than spiritual experiences and ecstatic forms of worship. Pentecostals have always stressed evangelism and regarded it as the primary task of all Christians—not of just a few key church members. They encouraged lay leadership long before it became fashionable in the historic churches. From the very beginning, with Charles Parham to the days at Azusa, there has been a fiery emphasis on reaching the world with the message of the Gospel. From the onset, the Pentecostal gospel has included personal salvation, Holy Spirit baptism, healing, and deliverance.

Their strong belief in the supernatural has been a powerful factor in their evangelism success and stands them in stark contrast to the rationalistic flow of the secular culture. The early Pentecostals and those today believe that the Pentecostal experience empowers them to overcome and enjoy spiritual victory. They were and are fervent in their belief that the baptism in the Spirit is for victory over sin and power over all the forces of darkness. Spirit baptism also brought a new dynamic of power that enabled them to serve the cause of Christ in a new and effective way.

But ye shall receive power, after that the Holy Ghost is come upon you: and ye shall be witnesses unto Me both in Jerusalem, and in all Judaea, and in Samaria, and unto the uttermost part of the earth (Acts 1:8 KJV).

The Growth of Pentecostalism

The Pentecostal movement is by far the largest and most important religious movement to originate in the United States. Beginning in 1901 with only a handful of students in a Bible school in Topeka, Kansas, and spreading west to Azusa Street in Los Angeles, the number of Pentecostals increased steadily throughout the world during the 20th century until by 1993 they had become the largest family of Protestants in the world.

Pentecostalism developed into an international missionary effort almost immediately, which spread first among ethnic communities in North America and quickly flowed to Europe. By the end of 1906, missionary work had begun in Norway; and in 1907 the movement reached the rest of Scandinavia and Germany, Italy, and Holland. Latinos who took part in the Azusa Street revival helped spread the movement to Mexico, and a vital Spanish-speaking church movement developed there and in the Southwestern region of the United States.

Pentecostal missionaries reached South Africa in 1907 and found a home in the mission established only a few years earlier by representatives of the Christian Catholic church, an American church that emphasized healing. They were joined in 1914 by Assemblies of God missionaries. Nicholas B.H. Bhengu, a former Lutheran who joined the Assemblies of God, was the first great African-born Pentecostal evangelist. With the emergence of the African Independent Church after World War II, Pentecostalism became a mass movement across the southern areas of Africa.

With over 200 million members designated as denominational Pentecostals, this group surpassed the Orthodox churches as the second largest denominational family of Christians, exceeded only by the Roman Catholics. In addition to these "classical denominational Pentecostals," there were over 200 million "charismatic" Pentecostals in the mainline denominations and independent charismatic churches, both Catholic and Protestant, placing the number of both Pentecostals and charismatics at well over 420 million people in 1993. This explosive growth has forced the Christian world to pay increasing attention to the entire movement and to attempt to discover the root causes of the growth. About 25 percent of the world's Christians are Pentecostal or charismatic—an estimated 450 million (See http://ctLibrary.com/ct/1998/November16/8td28a.html).

GOING BACK, IN ORDER TO GO BEYOND

Too often we forget the lessons of the past, and as we do, we eventually become trapped in the maze of a drifting culture, disconnected from the source of power that made us who we are. It is too easy to lose touch with all that made us significant and relevant. Therefore, there are times when we must get out of the forward flow of time and reflect backward in the hopes of capturing what we lost.

All of the Pentecostalism expressions of the 21st century can trace their beginnings to the Holy Spirit fire that fell at Azusa Street. And in order to find the secrets that spawned this revival of the Spirit, we must trace our steps back to the early days of the Church.

Stepping back even further in the Word, we will learn that what took place in the city of Jerusalem with a small band of Jews was replicated in the city of Los Angeles with a seemingly inconspicuous group of "Holy Rollers."

Chapter One

ROOTS OF REVIVAL

In the last days, God says, "I will pour out My Spirit on all people. Your sons and daughters will prophesy, your young men will see visions, your old men will dream dreams" (Acts 2:17).

THE real Pentecostal movement did not begin in the 20th century—it began in the first century, in the ancient city of Jerusalem, where we find the original well of Holy Spirit water that would eventually flow to the ends of the earth.

John the Baptist, who had initiated a revival of spiritual fervor among the Jewish people with his fiery preaching of repentance, told his Jewish audience that the One coming after him would baptize them with the Holy Spirit. Soon afterwards, at His baptism in the cool flowing waters of the Jordan, Jesus was identified as the coming One.

In John chapter 14, the small band of disciples who followed Jesus heard Him say toward the end of His ministry that it was expedient that He leave them; but when He did, He would not leave them alone. He would send the Holy Spirit who would come in a way that would guarantee the continuing presence of Jesus in the world of man.

After the resurrection, Jesus gathered His disciples together and gave them His final instructions. He did not give them a plan about how to build the Church nor did He offer them advice about how to win the world. He simply told them to gather together and wait for the promise of the Father, which would be an outpouring of the Spirit upon each of them. However, the disciples, not known for their ability to understand what Jesus was saying, asked Him when He would restore the Kingdom. Their minds were still focused on the glory that had been lost, and they were wondering when "paradise lost" would be restored.

Unwilling to be deterred by this theological sidetrack, He refocused their attention on His critical commands and said to them, *"It is not for you to know the times or dates which the Father has set by His own authority. But you will receive power when the Holy Spirit comes on you; and you will be My witnesses in Jerusalem, and in all Judea and Samaria, and to the ends of the earth"* (Acts 1:7-8). Then, before they had a chance to digress into another irrelevant thought, He was lifted up and taken out of their sight.

Waiting for the Holy Spirit

After a final reminder from the angels about what they were to do, the dazed disciples drifted back into the city heading toward the upper room. And there they waited. They had no idea what they were waiting for. They did not know who the Holy Spirit was, and they did not know what would happen when that Spirit would fall upon them. Huddled together in the upper room, they waited and they prayed; and as they prayed, they wondered what it would be like when He came.

And then it happened. A spiritual energy entered the room as heavenly winds swept in—the day of Pentecost had arrived. Everyone felt the sudden rush of a power invading their inner being, and suddenly, they were overwhelmed with a Presence that was—well, very familiar. It was Jesus. The Presence of Jesus gave them confidence as it filled the emptiness in their hearts. Tongues of fire were dancing above them, and strange words began to form in their spirit. What were these words? First there was a trickle, and then the trickle became a flood as louder and louder each disciple spoke in a heavenly language.

After drinking sip after sip from the cup of the Holy Spirit, they drifted down the stairs and stumbled into the streets, drunk with spiritual power and speaking in tongues.

As they submitted to the stream of strange sounds and words pouring out of their mouths, they noticed a gathering crowd. Some were ridiculing them while others were listening intently. In response, with courage and confidence, they boldly declared a glorious message concerning the Jewish Messiah. The rituals of animal sacrifices had ended and now forgiveness was offered to all who would trust the risen Lord, Jesus. On that day, the Church was born.

The Fire Fell, the Church Was Born

Under the power and direction of the Holy Spirit, the Church grew in numbers, and the sounds of the new Church were heard throughout the city. Along with these new sounds came new power—power to save, to deliver, to heal, and to serve.

To the amazement of the 120 Jews comprising the congregation, the power of the Spirit also fell on Gentiles. First the Spirit fell on those at Cornelius' house and then it spread to Antioch; and with the conversion and ministry of the apostle Paul, it impacted the entire Roman Empire. The fire that originally fell in Jerusalem proceeded to scorch the earth with the flame of the Holy Spirit.

Their meetings were filled with joy and enthusiasm as they worshiped the Lord and served one another, and the passion of their love for one another was the envy of the world. In addition, signs and wonders, miracles, and supernatural manifestations were dynamic characteristics of this young, fledgling Church.

The presence of the Holy Spirit and the preaching of the Word gave legitimacy to the primitive Church. Indeed, it was not an illegitimate birth produced by the inventiveness and initiative of man, and there was never a need for implementation of church-planting strategies or high-powered citywide crusades. Their activities were simply orchestrated by the movements of the Spirit in their midst.

The early Church continued to live in the power of that Spirit as manifested in the spontaneity of its actions, the vigor of its life, the dynamics of spiritual gifts, and the corporate witness of the living Lord to the world. They were utterly dependent on the Spirit for their personal and corporate life.

During this time, there was a synchronous movement between the directions of the Spirit and the actions of the little flock. The life of God resident in them found no hindrance as it flowed through them into the world around them. It was physically manifested in the authority of their words, the power of their actions, their love for one another, and the fellowship they had with Him. They were the first Pentecostals as evidenced through their experience of the gifts and the power of their worship.

Decline of the Early Church

As the Church turned the corner into the second century, there appears to be a suspension of the Spirit's dynamic because of a choice to trust the powers of man rather than being patient and waiting on the Holy Spirit. This temporary cessation of the gifts and the miraculous was not the result of the stopping of a dispensational time clock but the product of having lost touch with the dimension of the other realm—the realm where God lives, the realm of the Spirit. The early Pentecostals became mere mortals. Unfortunately, the "Church is where the Spirit is" became the "church where the bishop is." The order of man replaced the order of the Spirit, and the result was a break in the flow of Heaven's power flowing into the Church.

In the middle of the second century, Montanus appeared as a new prophet in Phrygia, and found many adherents. Alcibiades and Theodotus and later Tertullian were some of the well-known ones. Under Montanus, prophetesses also appeared—Priscilla and Maximilla.

Prophecy was, indeed, the most prominent feature of this new movement. Ecstatic visions, announcements about the approach of the second advent of Christ, and the establishment of the heavenly Jerusalem were prominent teachings among the Montanists. Unfortunately, they embraced a heavy form of legalism and spiritual pride that rendered them unable to sustain any kind of spiritual renewal.

With the coming of Constantine in the third century and the succeeding secularization of the church, the breach was completed, and the church was set adrift in an ocean of legalism, formalism, papalism, and traditionalism.

THE DESERT FATHERS AND THE MONASTIC ORDERS

As the church sailed into an ocean of legalism and ritualism, there was an emergence of monastic orders. In search of a deeper spirituality, some believers turned inward and took their pursuit to the deserts and the mountains—some forsaking riches and living among the poor—to seek the original wells of spirituality. "Christian monasticism began in the deserts of Egypt and Syria in fourth century a.d. The desert fathers, as they were called, sought to experience the realities of the Kingdom of Heaven. As they retreated from organized religion they sought to recover the simple ways of primitive Christianity. Abba Poemen said that Abba John said that the saints are like a group of trees, each bearing different fruit, but watered from the same source. The practices of one saint differ from those of another, but it is the same Spirit that works in all of them."[1]

Even though the gifts of the Spirit were hardly recognized, there were still pockets of Pentecostals. Evidently some "heretics" in Augustine's day believed in receiving the Holy Spirit with evidence of speaking in tongues. He sought to refute them with the following argument: (1) Tongues are valueless without love (1 Corinthians 13); (2) Love comes only by the Spirit (Romans 5:5); (3) They did not have the Spirit because they did not belong to the Catholic Church; and (4) No one expected tongues any longer anyway.[2]

Among the principal monastic orders that evolved in the Middle Ages were the Carthusians in the 11th century and the Cistercians in the 12th; the mendicant orders, or friars—Dominicans, Franciscans, and Carmelites—arose in the 13th century. These monastic orders were formed in opposition to the decline in spirituality in the church. Among the saints there was evidence of tongues and other manifestations of the Spirit such as:

- Hilary (died 367), bishop of Poitiers, mentioned both tongues and interpretation of tongues, describing them as "agents of ministry" ordained of God.[3]

- Ambrose (340-98), bishop of Milan, taught that all the gifts of First Corinthians 12 were part of the normal Christian experience.[4]

By the late fourth century and early fifth century, Christendom had for the most part evolved into what became known as the Roman Catholic Church. Apparently speaking in tongues had practically disappeared from most places in the backsliding church, but the memory of it remained to some extent. John Chrysostom (345-407), bishop of Constantinople, wrote a comment on First Corinthians 12:

This whole place is very obscure: but the obscurity is produced by our ignorance of the facts referred to and by their cessation, being such as then used to occur but now no longer take place.... Well: what did happen then? Whoever was baptized he straightway spoke with tongues.... They at once on their baptism received the Spirit... [They] began to speak, one in the tongue of the Persians, another in that of the Romans, another in that of the Indians, or in some other language. And this disclosed to outsiders that it was the Spirit in the speaker.[5]

There are rare evidences of speaking in tongues during the Middle Ages, probably because the Roman Catholic Church was so effective in silencing "heretics." Nevertheless, there are reports of speaking in tongues among the following three groups:

Waldenses, 1100s, Europe

Albigenses, 1100s, Europe

Franciscans, 1200s, Europe

St. Francis Xavier is said to have preached in tongues unknown to him; and St. Vincent Ferrer, while using his native tongue, was understood in others.[6]

MIRACLES AND THE MYSTICS

"Mysticism, according to its historical and psychological definitions, is the direct intuition or experience of God; and a mystic is a person who has, to a greater or less degree, such a direct experience—one whose religion and life are centered, not merely on an accepted belief or practice, but on that which the person regards as first hand personal knowledge" (Evelyn Underhill, *Mystics of the Church*[7]).

During the time of the great mystics of the church, there were credible reports of the operation of the Spirit as evidenced in amazing miracles, prophetic words, and many signs and wonders. In the lives of the mystics, Pentecost was preserved.

St. Anthony of Padua (d. 1231) has been given a number of impressive titles, some of which are "The Wonder-Worker of Padua," "Evangelical Doctor," and "The Hammer of Heretics." He is regarded as the first theologian of the Franciscan Order and has been numbered among the Doctors of the Church since 1946. Renowned as a worker of miracles, he was also acclaimed as a preacher. It is said that St. Anthony "...possessed in an eminent degree all the good qualities that characterized an eloquent preacher: a loud and clear voice, a winning countenance, wonderful memory, and profound learning, to which were added from on high the spirit of prophecy and an extraordinary gift of miracles." About the many miracles performed by the Saint before and after his death, one authority states that most of the miracles "came to us on such high authority that it is impossible either to eliminate them or explain them away without doing violence to the facts of history."[8]

St. Catherine of Cienna (d. 1380) was consumed by a dual passion of deep love for God and a wonderful compassion for the poor. As she pursued these passions, miracles followed.

"*St. Francis of Xavier* (d. 1552) is one of the Church's most productive and active missionaries. He was born of noble parents and was by nature refined, aristocratic and ambitious. While he was a professor at the University of Paris he met the renowned St. Ignatius Loyola. Their meeting developed into a lifelong friendship and Xavier would become one of Ignatius' original seven followers. His missionary career began in 1540, traveling to the East Indies. During a ten-year period of time he would travel to within to Ceylon, India, Malaya and Japan. It is record-ed in Catholic history that he 'performed many miracles and exercised many mystical gifts.'"[9]

Teresa of Availa (d. 1582) spearheaded a spiritual awakening in Spain and was blessed with a diversity of gifts—contemplation, miracle work-ing, and pastoral care.

Madam Guyon (d. 1717) recorded these words in her biography:

I was insatiable for prayer. I arose at four o'clock in the morn-ing to pray. I went very far to the church, which was so situat-ed, that the coach could not come to it. There was a steep hill to go down and another to ascend. All that cost me nothing; I had such a longing desire to meet with my God, as my only good, who on His part was graciously forward to give Himself to His poor creature, and for it to do even visible miracles.

Every day I saw new miracles, which both amazed and still more confirmed me; for with a paternal goodness Thou tookest care of even the smallest things.[10]

FIRES OF REFORMATION

Martin Luther

In 1510, Martin Luther was sent to Rome on business for his order, and there he was shocked by the spiritual laxity apparent in high ecclesiastical places.

Upon his return, he completed the work for his theological doctorate and became a professor at Wittenberg. This period was the beginning of the intimacy between Luther and John von Staupitz, whose influence led Luther to say in 1531, "I have received everything from Staupitz." For Luther these years were times of profound spiritual and physical torment. Obsessed with anxieties about his own salvation, he sought relief in frequent confession and extreme asceticism. His search for peace of mind led him, under the guidance of Staupitz, to further study of the Scriptures.

In preparation for his university lectures in 1513, especially on the letters of Paul, Luther finally resolved his turmoil. In the Scriptures, Luther found a loving God who bestowed upon sinful humans the free gift of salvation, to be received through faith, against which all good works were as nothing.

There is a tendency when thinking of the Reformation to think only of Calvinism and orthodoxy—not prophecy or prophetic utterance! In one sense the reformers were prophets calling the church into God's truth on a grand scale. When I speak of prophecy, I mean the manifestation of revelatory words, as Paul describes, as one of the nine gifts of the Spirit in First Corinthians chapters 12–14.

However, the Reformation was more than just a return to fresh revelation of the Scriptures. Martin Luther taught on the value of the prophetic in his commentary on Joel 2:28. "For what are all other gifts, however numerous they may be, in comparison with this gift, when the Spirit of God Himself, the eternal God, descends into our hearts, yea, into our bodies, and dwells in us, governs, guides, and leads us? Thus with respect to this declaration of the prophet, prophecy, visions and dreams are, in truth, one precious gift."

Although Luther was not a Pentecostal in the traditional sense of the word, he was a man who battled the devil and prayed for the sick. Once he found his bosom friend, Melanchthon, deathly sick. "While Luther looked at Melanchthon, deprived of sight, hearing, and unconscious, he exclaimed, 'God forbid! How has the devil disfigured this instrument?' Then he prayed a wonderful prayer in simple, child-like trust. He took Melanchthon by the hand and said: 'Be of good cheer, Philip, thou wilt not die. Give no place to the spirit of grief, nor become the slayer of thyself, but trust in the Lord, who is able to kill and to make alive.'" He began to revive, and afterward said that he would have been a dead man if he had not been recalled from death itself by the coming of Luther.[11]

"When Myconius, the superintendent at Gotha was in the last stage of consumption, Dr. Luther wrote him, 'May God not let me hear so long as I live that you are dead, but cause you to survive me. I pray this earnestly, and will have it granted. Amen.'" Myconius began at once to regain strength.[12]

One of the great contributions of the Reformation was the translation of the Scriptures into the language of the people. With the invention of the Guttenburg Press and these new translations, the Scriptures were made available to the "common" people; and as the Scriptures were made known, the Holy Spirit brought fresh revelation to them.

CAMISARDS

Following the Reformation, an amazing story of the "French Prophets" emerged. They are also known as "the little prophets of the Cevennes," named after the young age of those who prophesied and the Cevennes mountains where they hid from persecution.

There had been a halfhearted attempt at religious freedom for the Protestants in France since 1598 and the Edict of Nantes. However, in 1685 Louis XIV revoked the treaty and persecution returned. Like the Montanist movement, they experienced strong convulsions and ecstatic movements as the Word of the Lord was being proclaimed. To a large extent, this was the contentious issue with the French church and government. Thousands were martyred; many fled to England; others entrenched in the mountains. Those who attempted to defend themselves during the years 1701-1710 were called the "Camisards." Miracles, healings, tongues, and prophecy flowed in their meetings; and the anointing seemed to be very contagious.

One peasant named Halmede had a son 12 years old who had received this blessing. Yet it wasn't a blessing to the father who knew that many households were massacred for revealing such news. Meanwhile the local parish priest counseled that a forced fast with added beatings would stop his son from prophesying. But it was to no avail, and Halmede returned in a short while with the same complaint. The last hope offered was the use of a snakeskin as a charm, or amulet, which was to be placed over the boy's head when he began to shake and prophecy. However, when this remedy was used, the child was shaken with a violent trembling; and with a loud voice, he shouted out the displeasure of the Lord over the sinful act that the father was committing. Then, like a bolt of lightning, Halmede was struck and began to weep tears of repentance. Within a few days, he became like his son—a shaking prophet with the Spirit of revelation and knowledge.

So, we discover that the rise of the gift of prophecy is not confined to these last few decades. We are merely following in the path of other pioneers—some of them children. Have you witnessed child prophets in your midst?

The common manifestations of the "French Prophets" were: falling to the ground, groaning from the chest, the jerks, visions, prophesying in perfect French when patois was their only spoken language, and a host of other gifts of the Spirit and miracles. One man named Jean Cavalier testified that God's presence would often come upon him and he would experience "the jerks" and at times fall to the ground. This lasted for nine months until one Sunday morning prayer time in his house when God loosed his tongue and he prophesied after an extended period of shaking. Children as young as fourteen months prophesied the word of the Lord in impeccable Parisian French. They often spoke of the angelic song that would be heard in their meetings.[13]

ANABAPTISTS

Unlike many of the Reformers, the Anabaptists emphasized:

1. The restoration of apostolic patterns of worship and lifestyle,

2. The importance of a conversion experience,

3. Baptism of believers only,

4. Baptism by immersion,

5. Total separation of church and state,

6. The power to overcome sin after conversion, and

7. The need to live a holy life.

A prominent Anabaptist leader named Menno Simons, whose followers became known as Mennonites, wrote about speaking in tongues as if it were expected evidence of receiving the Holy Spirit.

Many early Anabaptists worshiped quite demonstratively; in the words of a secular history text some participated in "very excited, enthusiastic, evangelical practices...what Americans know as 'holy rolling'.... The congregation sometimes shouted and danced, and always sang hymns with great fervor."[14]

The Anabaptists, known as the radical wing of the Reformation, were not content with the emphasis on the sola scriptura (Scripture only) of Luther and Calvin. They claimed that the inward voice of the Holy Spirit takes precedence over the external Word of Scripture. Many reports of highly-charged gatherings, which included tongue-speaking, are recorded in Anabaptist literature.

MORAVIANS

In 1722, a small band of Bohemian peasants and craftsman crossed the German border and entered Czechoslovakia seeking refuge and religious liberty. They arrived at the estate of Count Zinzendorf and there a spiritual revival would occur that would eventually impact the world. "From the community of settlers there emerged in 1727 the renewed Moravian Church, a fusion of the older strain of the Unity with the dynamic revival spirit of Pietism."[15] Zinzendorf, who would eventually become the key leader, allowed them to settle on one of his estates. He was 27 years old, about the average age of the group.

Not many months after they started their community, the Moravian Brethren became conscious of a special nearness of God's presence.

On Wednesday, August 13, the church, dissatisfied with themselves, came together for a specially called communion service. "They had quit judging each other because they had become convinced, each one, of his lack of worth in the sight of God and each felt himself at this communion to be in view of the Saviour. They left that communion at noon, hardly knowing whether they belonged to earth or had already gone to Heaven. It was a day of outpouring of the Holy Spirit. 'We saw the hand of God and were all baptized with his Holy Spirit. The Holy Spirit came upon us and in those days and great signs and wonders took place in our midst.'"[16]

Count Zinzendorf of the Moravians

"Zinzendorf has been brought up under Pietistic influences, and out of the Moravian refugees and other followers he created a new society marked by a belief in salvation by faith, personal conversion as 'new birth,' and an intense personal devotion to Jesus Christ which at times took very sentimental and bizarre forms."

As a result of this spiritual awakening, the Moravians committed themselves to pray for the worldwide spread of the Gospel. They met in pairs to pray hour by hour around the clock, an "Hourly Intercession" which continued for more than one hundred years. It led to the launch of one of the most significant worldwide missionary efforts ever. Their first missionaries went to the West Indies to minister to slaves, willing to become slaves themselves, if necessary, to reach those in dismal servitude. Also, it was the Moravians who so influenced John Wesley and led to his life-changing "heart strangely warmed" Aldersgate experience, from which the Methodist movement exploded. The Wesleyan revival would become the spiritual forerunner of the modern Pentecostal and Charismatic movements.

JOHN WESLEY AND THE METHODISTS

John Wesley

John Wesley, in his journal entry for August 15, 1750, wrote, "I was fully convinced of what I had long suspected, 1. That the Montanists, in the second and third centuries, were real, scriptural Christians; and, 2. that the grand reason why the miraculous gifts were so soon withdrawn, was not only that faith and holiness were well nigh lost; but that dry, formal, orthodox men began even then to ridicule whatever gifts they had not themselves, and to decry them all as either madness or imposture."

Wesley clearly believed that the gifts of the Holy Spirit were relevant for the Church in any age. He defined them. He described them. He experienced them. He defended them.

Although Wesley never emphasized certain gifts, such as predictive prophecy or tongues and their interpretation, he did regret their loss to Christians in general. In his sermon, "The More Excellent Way," he writes,

> The cause of this [decline of spiritual gifts following Constantine] was not, (as has been vulgarly supposed,) "because there was no more occasion for them," because all the world was become Christians. This is a miserable mistake; not a twentieth part of it was then nominally Christian. The real cause was, "the love of many," almost of all Christians, so called, was "waxed cold." The Christians had no more of the Spirit of Christ than the other Heathens. The Son of Man, when he came to examine his Church, could hardly "find faith upon earth." This was the real cause why the extraordinary gifts of the Holy Spirit were no longer to be found in the Christian Church; because the Christians were turned Heathens again, and had only a dead form left.[17]

Wesley himself believed that the gifts of the Spirit had practically disappeared but that a fully restored Church would have them again.[18] When a certain Dr. Middleton wrote that the gift of tongues was absent from later church history, Wesley replied that (1) many ancient writings are no longer extant, (2) many Christians wrote no books, (3) the ante-Nicene fathers do not say tongues ceased with the apostles, and (4) just because tongues was not specifically recorded does not mean it was not practiced. He said, "Many may have spoken with new tongues, of whom this is not recorded; at least, the records are lost in a course of so many years."[19]

We should also note the strong emphasis on repentance and physical demonstrations in the Methodist revivals. One hostile historian wrote, "Extreme emotional disturbances, ecstasies and bodily seizures of various sorts were common in the Wesleyan Revival of the eighteenth century in England," with people in Wesley's meetings exhibiting "violent motor reactions… convulsions and shakings" and screaming. (See http://ourworld.compuserve.com/homepages/pentecostal/new-ch11.htm.)

Although there is no record that Wesley himself ever spoke in tongues, there is evidence that he believed that this gift of the Holy Spirit was a legitimate gift for the Church of any age. I offer but two quotations from his letter to Middleton.

In response to Middleton, Wesley writes: "Since the Reformation, you say, 'This gift has never once been heard of, or pretended to, by the Romanists themselves.' But has it been pretended to (whether justly or not) by no others, though not by the Romanists? Has it 'never once been heard of' since that time? Sir, your memory fails you again: It has undoubtedly been pretended to, and that at no great distance either from our time or country. It has been heard of more than once, no farther off than the valleys of Dauphiny. Nor is it yet fifty years ago since the Protestant inhabitants of those valleys so loudly pretended to this and other miraculous powers, as to give much disturbance to Paris itself. And how did the King of France confute that pretense, and prevent its being heard any more? Not by the pen of his scholars, but by (a truly heathen way) the swords and bayonets of his dragoons."

On the relevance of speaking in tongues, Wesley once more responds to Middleton: "'All these [spiritual gifts] worketh by one and the self-same Spirit, dividing to every man severally as he will;' and as to every man, so to every Church, every collective body of men…seeing He who worketh as He will, may, with your [Middleton's] good leave, give the gift of tongues, where He gives no other; and may see abundant reasons so to do, whether you and I see them or not. For perhaps we have not always known the mind of the Lord; not being of the number of his counselors" (Works, 10:56).[20]

Pentecostal historian Vinson Synan suggests that John Wesley and the emerging Methodist church was one of the strongest influences on the coming Pentecostal movement. "Perhaps the most important immediate precursor to Pentecostalism was the Holiness movement which issued from the heart of Methodism at the end of the Nineteenth Century. From John Wesley, the Pentecostals inherited the idea of a subsequent crisis experience variously called 'entire sanctification,' 'perfect love,' 'Christian perfection,' or 'heart purity.' It was John Wesley who posited such a possibility in his influential tract, A Plain Account of Christian Perfection (1766). It was from Wesley that the Holiness Movement developed the theology of a 'second blessing.' It was Wesley's colleague, John Fletcher, however, who first called this second blessing a 'baptism in the Holy Spirit,' an experience which brought spiritual power to the recipient as well as inner cleansing."[21]

The Great Awakening and the Holiness movement that would flow out of the Methodist movement would be the cradle of the coming Pentecostal movement in America.

ENDNOTES

1. http://www.cin.org/dsrtft20.html.

2. Augustine, *On Baptism*, Against the Donatists, 3.16.21, NPNF 1st ser., IV, 442.

3. Hilary, *On the Trinity*, 8.33, NPNF 2nd ser., IX, 147.

4. Ambrose, *Of the Holy Spirit*, 2.8, NPNF 2nd ser., X, 134.

5. John Chrysostom, *Homilies on First Corinthians*, 29, NPNF, 1st ser., XII, 168.

6. Catholic Encyclopedia,
   http://www.newadvent.org/cathen/14776c.htm.

7. http://www.christianmystics.com/

8. Catholic Encyclopedia,
   http://www.newadvent.org/cathen/01556a.htm.

9. http://www.tanbooks.com/doct/mysteries_marvels.htm.

10. Autobiography of Madame Guyon,
    http://www.believerscafe.com/autobiographyguyon.htm

11. http://www.biblebelievers.net/Charismatic/kjcheal8.htm

12. http://www.biblebelievers.net/Charismatic/kjcheal8.htm

13. http://www.godspeak.org/ps_lessons/ps6_week2.html

14. Crane Brinton et al., *A History of Civilization* 3rd ed. (Englewood Cliffs, NJ: Prentice-Hall, 1967), 480.

15. Donald Durnbaugh, *The Believers' Church* (New York: MacMillian Company, 1968), 63.

16. http://www.ucmpage.org/articles/rtuttle1.html

17. Howard, Snyder, *The Radical Wesley* (Downers Grove, IL: Intervarsity Press, 1980), 96.

18. John Wesley, "A Letter to the Reverend Dr. Conyers Middleton," The *Works of John Wesley*, 3rd. ed. (Rpt. Grand Rapids: Baker Book House, 1978), X, 54-55.

19. http://www.ucmpage.org/articles/rtuttle1.html

20. http://www.oru.edu/university/library/holyspirit/pentorg1.html

21.Williston Walker, *A History of the Christian Church* (New York: Scribner, 1918), 608.

Chapter Two

THE AWAKENING

THE GREAT AWAKENING

THE roots of "The Great Awakening," the most sweeping and transforming movement of the 18th century, extend back to both the Wesleyan movement in England and the Pietist revivals in Europe. Formalism and spiritual lethargy have always been the seedbed for revival, and The Great Awakening was a reaction to the fact that the church had drifted into a dead state of formalism and had experienced a loss of spiritual vitality. Early signs of the imminent fire of revival eruption can be traced back to Dutch Reformed congregations in the Raritan valley of New Jersey. A young pastor, Theodore Relinghuysen, who had become acquainted with Puritan emphasis and experiences while studying in Holland, challenged his church to pursue a more personal, intimate experience with God. A little fire of revival was breaking out, and many were being attracted to the light and warmth. Although there were those opposed to the emotional intensity of the revival, it was too late. The fire was falling.

The key leaders in the Awakening were William Tennet, a Presbyterian pastor affected by the revival in New Jersey; George Whitefield, whose dynamic preaching created a fire everywhere he preached; and Jonathan Edwards, the most notable of the three. The vibrant preaching of Whitefield during his tours to America created an environment in which the fire of revival could spread. Tennet, and mainly Edwards, then fanned the flame into a blaze that would last for half a century.

Jonathan Edwards

"The Great Awakening reached New England when a remarkable revival swept the town of Northhampton, Massachusetts, in 1734-1735. It attracted great attention, especially when its leader, Jonathan Edwards, Congregational pastor, described it in a revivalist classic, *A Faithful Narrative of the Surprising Work of God in the Conversion of Many Hundred Souls...*"[1]

Edwards preached with a forceful presentation of the Gospel and a determined faith that found its source in his own spiritual encounters with God, leaving an indelible mark upon his soul and influencing every word he spoke.

Once, as I rode out into the woods for my health, in 1737, having alighted from my horse in a retired place, as my manner commonly has been, to walk for divine contemplation and prayer, I had a view, that for me was extraordinary, of the glory of the Son of God, as mediator between God and man, and his wonderful, great, full, pure and sweet grace and love, and meek and gentle condescension. This grace, that appeared so calm and sweet, appeared also great above the heavens.[2]

Edwards' commanding, extemporaneous preaching stirred his audiences everywhere he traveled. His messages were so vivid, as well as convicting, that people would often fall to the ground or make unusual noises. There would be weeping and laughing and people acting like they were drunk. The Spirit fell with such great power that it set the stage for spreading the revival to Cane Ridge in Kentucky.

THE SECOND GREAT AWAKENING— CANE RIDGE REVIVAL AND CHARLES FINNEY

"Barton Stone, at the invitation of Daniel Boone, preached and served at the Cane Ridge Meeting House in Bourbon County. Stone was so overwhelmed by the Red River revival that he went home and, in May, 1801, called for a similar meeting in Cane Ridge, 'which was attended with blessing.' A second meeting, a six-day camp meeting in August, was then called; to the utter astonishment of all, over 20,000 people arrived for the six-day camp meeting!"[3] Among the thousands converted was the skeptic, James B. Finley, who later became a Methodist circuit rider. Here is his description in his own memorable words:

"The noise was like that of Niagara. The vast sea of human beings seemed to be agitated as if by a storm. I counted seven ministers, all preaching on stumps, others in wagons and one standing on a tree which had in falling, lodged against another.... Some of the people were singing, others praying, some crying for mercy in the most piteous accents, while others were shouting most vociferously. While witnessing these scenes, a peculiarly strange sensation such as I had never felt before came over me. My heart beat tumultuously, my knees trembled, my lips quivered and I felt as though I must fall to the ground. A supernatural power seemed to pervade the entire mass of mind there collected.... I stepped up on a log where I could have a better view of the surging sea of humanity. The scene that had presented itself to my mind was indescribable. At one time I saw at least five hundred swept down in a moment as if a battery of a thousand guns had been opened upon them and then immediately followed shrieks and shouts that rent the very heavens." (See http://www.spiritjournals.org/revivalfire/revivals/caneridgerevival.htm)

School House, Cane Ridge Revival

In an interview on the "700 Club" television show, Dr. Elmer Towns from Liberty College gave his own overview of the revival. "Cane Ridge was in Kentucky in 1800. It started at a communion service and it began with a Presbyterian serving communion. It was kind of a community communion service and a woman had a manifestation of the Holy Spirit.

"These extraordinary services exploded into the Cane Ridge camp meeting. The fiery preaching started at sun up and didn't stop until well into the night. Many people fell to their faces as the weight of their sins struck them cold. Others sang and danced as they felt the presence of God in their midst. Thousands flocked to Cane Ridge to experience a touch from God." (See http://www.700club.com/700club/scottross/commentary/for_caneridge.asp)

Barton Stowe, the key figure at the revival, described what he saw with these words:

> The scene to me was new and passing strange…Many, very many fell down, as men slain in battle, and continued for hours together in an apparently breathless and motionless state— sometimes for a few moments reviving, and exhibiting symptoms of life by a deep groan, or piercing shriek, or by a prayer for mercy most fervently uttered…though only a minority fell, some parts of the grounds were strewn like a battlefield.[4]

The Second Great Awakening had begun.

Twenty years after Cane Ridge, another new figure came on the scene extending this revival of spiritual passion. It was Charles G. Finney, a young lawyer who was convicted by the Holy Spirit, and like Martin Luther, his life was impacted while reading the Book of Romans.

> Without any expectation of it, without ever having the thought in my mind that there was any such thing for me, without the recollection that I had ever heard the thing mentioned by any person in the world, the Holy Spirit descended upon me in such a manner that seemed to go through me, body and soul. I could feel the impression, like a wave of electricity, going through and through me. Indeed it seemed to come in waves of liquid love; for I could not express it in any other way. It seemed like the very breath of God. I can recollect distinctly that it seemed to fan me, like immense wings. No words can express the wonderful love that was shed abroad in my heart.
>
> I wept aloud with joy and love; and I do not know but I should say I literally bellowed out the unutterable gushings of my

heart. These waves came over and over me, one after the other, until I cried out, "I shall die if these waves continue to pass over me." I said, "Lord, I cannot bear any more;" yet I had no fear of death. [5]

Charles G. Finney

Charles Finney's definition of sanctification was not associated with sinless perfection but manifested itself in perfect trust and consecration that resulted in social action. In Finney's theology, revivalism, holiness, and reform merged to form a single entity.[6]

EDWARD IRVING AND THE APOSTOLIC CHURCH

This same era saw the emerging of Edward Irving (1792-1834), former Scottish Presbyterian minister, and the founder of the Catholic Apostolic church. Irving was a charismatic preacher who was born in Annan (Dumfries and Galloway) and educated at the University of Edinburgh. He became a schoolmaster and in 1819 was appointed assistant to theologian Thomas Chalmers (1780-1847), who was later a leader of the Disruption in the Church of Scotland. Irving moved to London in 1822, becoming minister of the Caledonian Church in Covent Garden. Being convinced that the second coming of Jesus Christ was imminent, he preached and wrote on the subject. Within nine months, the congregation grew from 50 to more than 1,000. Subsequently, a ticket system was introduced because the building was designed to hold only 500. People from all walks of life flocked to hear him denounce the evils of his day. Later, in 1824, he and his congregation moved to a new church in Regent Square, which was then the largest in London, where prayer meetings were held for God to pour out His Spirit. Soon, speaking in tongues and interpretations were a regular occurrence.

School House, Cane Ridge Revival

"Unfortunately, like the Montanists, the Irvingites also had their share of charismatic idiosyncrasies. By 1835, they had established 12 apostles, and by 1836, they had organized all Christendom into '12 tribes' with an apostle for each apostolate, in anticipation of the imminent return of the Lord."[7]

"He was accused of heresy by the London Presbytery when he developed his views on Christ as a sinner and ejected from his charge, and the Church of Scotland, in 1833. Many of his congregation remained loyal to their pastor and this led to the formation of the Catholic Apostolic or Irvingite Church, although Irving's death limited his influence on the development of the new church. Today, the Apostolic Church claims around 8 million members world-wide (1994)."[8]

PHOEBE PALMER (D. 1874)

Phoebe Palmer

Phoebe Palmer was born in 1807 and is considered to be "The Mother of the Holiness Movement." This movement began in 1835 with her Tuesday Meetings for the Promotion of Holiness, which continued for 39 years in New York City, where she lived with her physician husband. The success of Phoebe Palmer's informal meetings encouraged other women to conduct the same type of ministry, and dozens of them sprang up throughout North America. Although Palmer was already inspiring many women around the country 13 years before the Womens' Rights Movement began, the church, unfortunately, did not understand the prophetic nature of her actions to encourage and empower women for the ministry.

"She could have graced a throne, or filled the office of a bishop, or organized and governed a new sect.... Whoever promotes holiness in all this country, must build upon the deep-laid foundations of this holy woman," wrote a leading minister upon the death in 1874 of Phoebe Palmer (See http://www.messiah.edu/whwc/articles/articles26.htm). A century later, M.E. Dieter argued in his history of *The Holiness Revival of the Nineteenth Century* that "the quiet discourse and boundless activity" of Mrs. Palmer "became the major impetus in setting off a world wide [holiness] movement."[9]

She became interested in the Wesleyan doctrine of Christian perfection; and professing with her husband the experience of "entire sanctification," held weekly meetings at her home for the advancement of this doctrine for nearly 50 years. They traveled extensively in this country and in Europe supporting their views. She was also an editor of a monthly magazine titled, The Guide to Holiness, and she was the author of: *The Way of Holiness* (New York, 1845); *Entire Devotion* (1845); *Faith and its Effects* (1846); *Incidental Illustrations of the Economy of Salvation* (1852); *Promises of the Father* (1856); *Four Years in the Old World* (1865); *Pioneer Experiences* (1867); and *Sweet Mary; or A Bride made ready for her Lord* (England, 1862).

John Fletcher, Wesley's lieutenant, was the first theologian to equate the experience of entire sanctification with the baptism of the Holy Spirit given at Pentecost. William Arthur, in his book, *The Tongue of Fire*, also equated sanctification with experiencing the Holy Spirit. Phoebe Palmer was impacted by Fletcher's thoughts and Pentecostal style language began to appear in her speaking and writing. During a four-year trip to promote the revival in England, Mrs. Palmer and her husband developed an order of service based on Pentecost which later became their standard pattern. They would start by leading a hymn about Pentecost, then have Dr. Palmer read and comment upon Acts 2. Next Mrs. Palmer would exhort those present to be baptized with "an inward baptism of pure fire." Those wishing to receive the blessing would then come forward for a prayer service around the altar, after which they would be urged to bear testimony about what the Lord had done for them.[10]

This connection between sanctification and the baptism of the Holy Spirit would be one of the great focuses of the coming Pentecostal revival at Azusa.

Palmer never claimed to be a preacher; she viewed much of the preaching of the day to be "metaphysical hair-splitting," "oratorical displays," and "pulpits of pedestal eminence."[11] She stood behind a pulpit, expounded on biblical topics, and drew larger crowds than most of the male preachers with whom she shared meetings. But she perceived that what she did was not preaching, but merely explaining, edifying, exhorting, and comforting from Scripture. A fellow preacher wrote, "She was unique and peculiar, not copying anyone's style, yet possibly reminding one of Mr. Wesley whom she so admired. I shall never forget the effect produced on both head and heart. Breathless attention was given so that not a word might be lost."[12]

Not even Palmer herself could deny her ability as a revivalist. Her speaking, whether called preaching or not, is said to have won more than 25,000 converts in the United States, some 17,300 in Britain, and several thousand more in Canada. Her answer to the success of her campaigns would again be a simple "Holiness is power!" Phoebe never sought fame. All that she ever wanted was to experience Holy Spirit power.

One of the many women stirred by Palmer's example was Mrs. Amanda Smith (1837-1915). Smith, an African-American, born a slave in Maryland, eventually gained her freedom, and in 1869 said she was called to preach. While an experience of sanctification in 1868 led to Smith's first hesitant attempts at preaching, by 1869 she was preaching regularly in African-American churches in New York and New Jersey after her husband and children had died. Smith's success in preaching before a white audience at a holiness camp meeting in the summer of 1870 led her to commit herself entirely to evangelism. She traveled widely over the next eight years, and in 1878 she sailed for England, where she spent a year evangelizing at holiness meetings. From 1879 to 1881 she was in India, and after another brief stay in England she sailed in 1881 for West Africa. For eight years she did missionary work in Liberia and Sierra Leone. Following another sojourn in Great Britain in 1889-90, she returned to the United States. She preached in eastern cities until 1892, when she moved to Chicago. Before long she had become a popular preacher at holiness camp meetings. Ten years later she went to India as a missionary, then to Liberia, an African country colonized mostly by ex-slaves from the United States. She also did evangelistic work in England, Ireland, and Scotland.[13]

After Palmer's death, and during the last years of Amanda Smith's life, the Holiness revival they both helped generate began to produce many new, independent churches.

HOLINESS MOVEMENT

The Holiness movement began within Methodism in the United States among those churches that felt they had lost the zeal and emphasis on personal holiness. During the latter part of the 19th century, as revival meetings were being attended by thousands, the National Holiness Camp Meeting Association was established in Vineland, New Jersey (1867) and went on to plant many Holiness camp meetings across the nation. The movement maintained its strength from the 1830s to the 1870s as they sought a deeper walk with God in what they called the second blessing of sanctification—also called the baptism in the Holy Spirit.

After 1875, the American Holiness movement, influenced by the Keswick emphasis, began to stress the Pentecostal aspects of the second blessings. Hence, the Keswick movement was critical to the development of the Pentecostal movement from where the movement got its emphasis on premillennialism and the baptism of the Holy Spirit. They created an atmosphere that was heavy with hope for a new Pentecost.

It was the Holiness writers who produced many of the hymns of the early Pentecostal movement, songs that celebrated the second blessing as both a cleansing and an empowering force. It was the Keswick teachers who made the shift in the purpose of this "second blessing" from "heart purity" to empowerment. Before the Pentecostal outpouring that started in 1901, there had already been a century of preachers who were teaching this second blessing.

R.A. Torrey, A.B. Simpson, Dwight L. Moody, and A.J. Gordon were some of the more conservative voices in the Keswick Movement, and all of these preachers claimed that they had been baptized in the Spirit, although there was no emphasis on tongues in their preaching.

Within the Holiness movement, there was also a radical wing that produced some of the earlier expressions of Pentecostal reality. "Southern California was a center of Holiness extremism. Bishop Alma White's 'Pillar of Fire' movement, which had its center in Denver, Colorado, and was best known for its practice of 'marching in the Spirit' had considerable appeal in Los Angeles and the surrounding towns. The 'Burning Bush' movement, which began in the independent Metropolitan Church in Chicago, was active in the same locale."[14]

Meanwhile, in the southern Appalachians, a small group of Baptists, calling themselves the Christian Union, experienced a revival in 1896. "Spiritually starved souls crowded into the one-room schoolhouse at Camp Creek, North Carolina, to join in weeping, shouting, trance, and ecstasy. Later, in prayer meetings of layman William Bryant, speaking in tongues and miracles of healing were reported to have taken place."[15]

JOHN ALEXANDER DOWIE

John Dowie and his wife, Jeannie

Born May 25, 1847, in Edinburgh, Dowie moved with his family to Australia as a boy, but later returned to Edinburgh to study theology. As a pastor, he then entered the Congregational ministry in 1870 in Alma, Australia, and spent the next several years campaigning against the use of tobacco and alcohol. During a personal experience of healing, he developed an interest in spiritual healing and eventually founded the International Divine Healing Association.

Sometime later a plague broke out in the city where Dowie was serving as pastor. At one point, after he became weary of all the death in his congregation, he looked to God to heal one of the members of his church; and from that time on, no one else in his congregation died from the plague. However, after this event, John didn't preach divine healing; he simply continued on as before.

A desire then began to grow within Dowie to go to America, and after praying about the matter, he and his family packed up and moved in the summer of 1886. Upon arriving in San Francisco, he started talking to people about the enduement of power from on high. John continued to minister in California for some time and then went to Chicago; and it was there that God used Dowie to do a great work among the people.

He built a small building close to the entrance of the world's fair in Chicago and dubbed it "the little wooden hut." After preaching there for a little while, he and his work were blessed by God and it grew. Later, he began to pastor in a large building, preaching against any and all types of vise. However, this message did not make him popular, and a great persecution presented itself against Dowie. In fact, he was arrested on false charges over 100 times in the course of one summer.

"During the year 1894, Dr. Dowie began the publication of a weekly periodical called *The Leaves of Healing*, which he fondly spoke of, as *The Little White Dove*. There had been some early issues published at more or less irregular intervals, but in 1894, it became a regular publication, and through it Dr. Dowie's sermons and writings became available to readers all over the world."[16] However, during this same time, he had his third-class mail certificate revoked, and many other similar things occurred. His persecutors, in an attempt to block the spread of this publication, had found a willing ally in the Chicago postmaster and for a time had removed his third-class postage privilege. But Dowie prevailed and his mailing privileges were restored.

"Against hypocritical opposing clergy, fierce and slanderous tabloids, murderous mobs, and relentless officials, Dr. Dowie wore his apostolic calling as a crown from God, and his persecution as a badge of honor."[17]

Once while working very late, which was his habit, he heard a voice telling him to get up and leave his office in the church. The next time he heard the voice, he got up and left the building. Only moments later the building exploded—dynamite had been planted right under his desk. God had taught him the value of hearing and obeying His voice.

In 1896, he founded the Christian Catholic Church, which emphasized spiritual healing but otherwise differed little from the more millennialist of the Protestant churches. In the meantime,

Dowie started to dream of building a city in which only Christians would live, a city where no vice or sin of any kind would be allowed. He called this city "Zion," and in order to bring his dream to reality, he dressed up like a tramp, and wandered the countryside buying up land—enough land to build a city. Finally, in 1900, he announced his undertaking to his congregation, and soon his city was built.

In 1901, Dowie established the City of Zion on the shore of Lake Michigan, about 40 miles north of Chicago, with about 5,000 of his followers. There was little or no persecution, and the walls of his new tabernacle were covered with braces, wheel chairs, and all types of apparatus for the lame and crippled—hung there by those Divinely healed!

Shiloh Temple, Zion city, Illinois

He ruled the community as a theocracy, forbidding physicians' offices, dance halls, theatres, drugstores, and smoking and drinking. Various industries were begun and the town prospered—with Dowie in sole control of the businesses. Zion's commercial success was increasingly jeopardized, however, by Dowie's several expensive and futile trips, first to New York to convert the city in 1903 and next to Mexico to establish the "Zion Paradise Plantation."

After all his success, trouble began. First, John began wearing priestly garments of his own design; then he started saying he was "Elijah." After this declaration, he seemed to have lost touch with reality. He tried to buy land to build other Zion Cities but in the process bankrupted the first one. Many other tragic events took place, and eventually, a great man of God fell, ironically, when the persecution stopped, although he had previously weathered all sorts of trials. When prosperity came to him in America, he abandoned his simple ways and pride filled his heart.

Opposition to his fiscal irresponsibility and other accusations led to his removal in 1906, and he was replaced by Wilbur Voliva, a trusted friend whom he had earlier named temporary head of the church. "Dowie suffered a stroke on the platform which he delivered his last sermon. Then while he was out of the country to recover, the City of Zion held an organizational meeting to vote Dowie out.

"Dowie fought this decision to the last ounce of his strength but never succeeded in regaining his position. He was allowed to live his last days inside of Shiloh House, his home of many years, and slipped into eternity on March 9, 1907."[18]

Out of the Dowie movement came a host of zealous Pentecostal converts who joined with those from Los Angeles and the lower Midwest in planting the movement among Holiness people in Chicago and beyond.[19] The Pentecostal message was then spread to Africa by John G. Lake, who had been an elder under Dowie. Among the many others who were also blessed and influenced by the ministry of Dr. Dowie were: F.F. Bosworth, Raymond T. Richey, Gordon Lindsay, Charles Parham, William H. Piper, Zion's Overseer At Large, who later became founder and pastor of the old Stone Church in Chicago, Fred Vogler, and J. Roswell Flower who was instrumental in the founding of the Assemblies of God in 1914.

MARIA WOODWORTH-ETTER

Maria Woodworth-Etter

In 1880, at the age of 35, Evangelist Maria Woodworth-Etter, a forerunner to the coming Pentecostal movement, began her dynamic ministry. Even though few women were in the pulpit at the time, like Phoebe Palmer, Maria didn't doubt her call and joined other women of that century to rise above the male prejudice against women in ministry.

In her earlier ministry, Maria emphasized conversions and was very successful in meetings sponsored by Methodists, United Brethren, and other groups. Then in 1883, people in her meetings began going into trances similar to what had happened in the Early Frontier meetings.

She was soon dubbed the "Trance Evangelist," though she believed the experience was the baptism in the Holy Spirit or "receiving the power." "The trances became the talk of the town. Hundreds flocked to taste of this outpouring, while others went to observe or ridicule."[20] During an 1883 meeting in Fairview, Ohio, Maria wrote that the people confessed sin and "prayed for a baptism of the Holy Spirit and of fire."

Fifteen people came to the altar screaming for mercy and fell over in trances. Even at that early date, Maria called it "the Pentecostal power," declaring "these outpourings of the Holy Ghost were always followed by hundreds coming to Christ."

In a large meeting in Alexandria, Indiana, Maria reported that the power of God took control of about 500 of the 25,000 people, causing many to fall to the ground. "The Holy Ghost sat upon them," she wrote. "I was overpowered." The pages of her memoirs are filled with examples of the most amazing manifestations of the Spirit.

> The power of God fell on the multitude...many fell to the ground. Others stood with their faces and hands raised to heaven. The Holy Ghost sat upon them. Others shouted, some talked, others wept. Others were converted, and began to testify and praise God. I was overpowered and carried to my tent.[21]

By 1885, she had developed a theology that included salvation, holiness, the baptism in the Holy Spirit, healing, and the imminent return of Christ. She was also big on prophecies—part of the excitement that helped fill an 8,000-seat tent from city to city. An 1887 newspaper quoted Maria in an Illinois meeting, giving her a powerful voice before the beginning of the Pentecostal movement, and by 1894, she had preached coast to coast at least three times. The power which was given to the apostles in their day had never been taken from the church. The trouble was, the churches had sunk to the level of the world and were without the unlimited faith that will heal the sick and make the lame to walk. She prayed for the return of the old days and more faith in Christ among the people.

> Before Sister Etter went home to be with the Lord at age eighty, she had buried all six of her children and two husbands; preached thousands of sermons from coast to coast; remained the victor over hoodlums and vicious ministers; blazed the trail for women

in ministry; and unflinchingly displayed the power of the Holy spirit with mighty sounds and wonders following.[22]

CHARLES MASON

Charles Harrison Mason

Charles Harrison Mason, who later became the founder and organizer of the Church of God in Christ (the largest African-American denomination in the world), was born September 8, 1866, near Memphis, Tennessee. His parents were converted during the dark days of American slavery, and he was converted in November 1878 and baptized by his brother, I.S. Nelson, a Baptist preacher. Fifteen years later, in 1893, Mason began to minister after accepting ministerial licenses from the Mt. Gale Missionary Baptist Church in Preston, Arkansas.

In the year 1893, Mason also became a student at Arkansas Baptist College on November 1, which was a short-lived experience—he stayed only three months and left after becoming dissatisfied with the methods of teaching and the presentation of the Bible message. He then returned to preaching and accepted every invitation afforded him.

While in Jackson, Mississippi, in 1896, Mason conducted a revival, which had enormous affects on the city. The spiritual manifestations of this revival, including the large numbers who were converted, sanctified, and healed by the power of faith, and the powerful teachings of Mason on the doctrine of sanctification, caused church doors within the Baptist association to close to him and to all those who believed and supported his teachings. As previously noted, everywhere the Pentecostal fire broke out there were those who became detractors and agitators standing against God's move of the Spirit.

At one point, Mason established a church in a gin house, the first meetinghouse for the church that would become the largest African-American denomination in the world. In 1897, while seeking a spiritual name that would distinguish this church from others of the similar title, Bishop Mason received a revelation—the church would be called "Church of God in Christ."

A turning point in Mason's life came in March 1907 when he journeyed to Los Angeles, California, to attend the great Pentecostal revival that everybody was talking about—the Azusa Revival. As he entered the little mission on Azusa Street, he heard Brother Seymour preaching from Luke 24:49, *"And behold I send the promise of My Father upon you; but tarry ye in the city of Jerusalem until ye be endued with power from on high."* Mason became convinced that it was essential for him to have the outpouring of the Holy Spirit.

The following excerpts are from Elder Mason's personal testimony regarding his receiving the Holy Spirit.

> The first day in the meeting I sat to myself, away from those that went with me. I began to thank God in my heart for all things, for when I heard some speak in tongues, I knew it was right though I did not understand it. Nevertheless, it was sweet to me.
>
> I also thank God for Elder Seymour who came and preached a wonderful sermon. His words were sweet and powerful and it

seems that I hear them now while writing. When he closed his sermon, he said "All of those that want to be sanctified or baptized with the Holy Spirit, go to the upper room; and all those that want to be justified, come to the altar." I said that is the place for me, for it may be that I am not converted and if not, God knows it and can convert me....The second night of prayer I saw a vision. I saw myself standing alone and had a dry roll of paper in my mouth trying to swallow it. Looking up towards the heavens, there appeared a man at my side. I turned my eyes at once, then I awoke and the interpretation came.

God had me swallowing the whole book and if I did not turn my eyes to anyone but God and Him only, He would baptize me. I said yes to Him, and at once in the morning when I arose, I could hear a voice in me saying, "I see..."I got a place at the altar and began to thank God. After that, I said Lord if I could only baptize myself, I would do so; for I wanted the baptism so bad I did not know what to do. I said, Lord, You will have to do the work for me; so I turned it over into His hands.

Then, I began to ask for the baptism of the Holy Ghost according to Acts 2:4, which readeth thus: "Then they that gladly received His word were baptized," then I saw that I had a right to be glad and not sad.

The Spirit came upon the saints and upon me...Then I gave up for the Lord to have His way within me. So there came a wave of Glory into me and all of my being was filled with the Glory of the Lord.

So when He had gotten me straight on my feet, there came a light which enveloped my entire being above the brightness of the sun. When I opened my mouth to say Glory, a flame touched my tongue which ran down me. My language changed and no word could I speak in my own tongue. Oh! I was filled with the Glory of the Lord. My soul was then satisfied.[23]

Under Mason's spiritual and apostolic direction, this church has grown from ten congregations in 1907, to the second largest Pentecostal group in America. The membership of the Church of God in Christ grew from 3 million in 1973 to an estimated 8 million in 1997.

THE CHRISTIAN UNION AND
THE SHEARER SCHOOLHOUSE REVIVAL—1896

"William Bryant, a layman, living in Cherokee County, North Carolina gave this description of the Shearer Schoolhouse Revival. Some of the worshipers were so enraptured with the One to whom they prayed that they were curiously exercised by the Holy Spirit, speaking in languages unknown to those who heard the ecstatic utterances." This revival took place near the Tennessee/North Carolina border. (See www.joyfulministry.com/penthist.htm)

Another participant in the revival was Richard G. Spurling, a Baptist Church pastor in Cokercreek, Monroe County, Tennessee. Spurling was concerned about traditionalism, legalism, and the declining church and called a conference in 1886 at the Barney Creek Meetinghouse. A union was formed to reassert the intrinsic doctrines of the Bible and the vital matters of Christian service, to restore primitive Christianity and bring about the union of all denominations. "Eight persons responded and came forward, desiring to be free from all man-made creeds and traditions and willing to take the New Testament for their only rule of faith and practice." (See www.churchofGod.cc/about/history.cfm)

Spurling died shortly after the Christian Union was formed; his son then took over and traveled by foot in Tennessee and North Carolina, "preaching to individuals he met in the way, debating with antagonistic preachers, praying and weeping constantly, winning what few converts he could." (See www.joyfulministry.com/penthist.htm)

At the same time, in Camp Creek, Cherokee County, North Carolina, a group of Baptists began to meet in their homes for prayer, singing, and testimonies. The "three" found their way there and the revival began. Using the Shearer Schoolhouse, they spoke from the Scriptures and their experience, with much prayer and fasting. The meetings began with singing, then testimonies, then prayer, with everyone praying aloud all at once; then followed the discourse and an altar call. People came from 15 to 30 miles away.

The people felt a strange exaltation that intermittently over-flowed in weeping and shouting. Their emotional expression frequently became even more demonstrative, for many danced with great joy as they were deeply moved by a sense of salvation and well-being.

Crowds grew, many were healed; the opposition began to form. However, a major feature of this movement was the burden of evangelism. There was a sense of immediacy and urgency in reaching beyond the confines of the mountains with the gospel of redemption, holiness, and the Spirit filled life. Following reports of revivals conducted during the past year was a period of consecration for evangelism during the coming year. The session was a time of much weeping so heavy lay the passion for souls upon their hearts. (See www.joyfulministry.com/penthis.htm)

THE WELSH REVIVAL

With all revivals there is a prelude to the kiss of divine favor that erupts in the manifestation of God's presence among His people. There were already signs of revival among the Welsh people, but the coming of Evan Roberts catapulted the revival movement into its popular phase. "The course of the Revival under the leadership of Mr. Evan Roberts in South Wales is irresistible. It overshadowed everything else. Its reports made up the chief feature in the South Wales daily press for many months. There was no building large enough to contain the crowds."[24]

Evan Roberts

Evan was an intensely humble, deeply spiritual, and extremely passionate young man. He gave himself to prayer and intercession, asking the Lord to baptize him in the Holy Spirit. While attending a meeting with the Rev. Seth Joshua, Roberts began to cry out, "Bend me, bend me." "In this prayer of total submission, he received a revelation of the love of God. Evan surrendered to the will of God that day and allowed His compassion to fill him. One of Evan's friends described him during this period as a 'particle of radium whose fire in their midst was consuming.'"[25]

In October 31, 1904, he launched a series of meetings that would last for two weeks and then quickly spread to the rest of the world. Roberts was not the typical preacher of his time. Instead of standing behind a pulpit and preaching a sermon, he would often walk up and down the aisles, preaching and asking questions of those sitting in the pews. Some of the meetings would last until 4 a.m., and as the people marched out, there would be crowds gathering for the 6 a.m. prayer meeting.

As it was with Seymour, Roberts was an extremely humble man, refusing to be seen as the leader of the revival and rarely allowing himself to be photographed. It was this humility that drew the people; and once there, they would come under the awesome manifestation of God's presence. It was a supernatural experience to be in one of his meetings. He carried a unique ability to steer the presence of God into a meeting. Roberts rarely preached and was most comfortable when all were singing and worshiping God. Praise was dominant, but prayer was always right behind. One of the features of the revival was the audible praying of many at the same time, and yet the sound of the rise of this audible prayer created no confusion. Many of God's children were refreshed and revived, and thousands were being saved. An American observer said that, "in the Welsh revival there is no preaching, no order, no hymn-books, no organs, no collections and no advertising."[26]

> A sense of the Lord's presence was everywhere. It pervaded, nay, it created the spiritual atmosphere. It mattered not where one went the consciousness of the reality and nearness of God followed. Felt, of course, in the Revival gatherings, it was by no means confined to them; it was also felt in the homes, on the streets, in the mines and factories, in the schools, yea, and even in the theatres and drinking saloons.[27]

It is estimated that over 100,000 were converted to Christ. Roberts said that there was no secret to this revival. It was simply, "Ask and ye shall receive."

Under a firestorm of criticism in 1905, the Welsh revival eventually began to diminish. Every revival in the history of world has had its critics and detractors. It is much easier to stand on the sidelines and throw your verbal spears than it is to thrust yourself totally into God's holy work. Winkie Pratney, in his book on revival, said that the end of Evan

Roberts' public ministry was "one of the strangest endings of a ministry in history."[28]

In the spring of 1906, Mr. and Mrs. Penn-Lewis sequestered the beleaguered Evan Roberts at their home in Leicestershire where they coauthored the book, *War on the Saints*. It is clear that as one studies the developing relationship between Mrs. Penn-Lewis and Evan Roberts that she eventually brought great confusion to his mind concerning the miraculous events of the Welsh revival. "This newly-formed team of Roberts and Penn-Lewis also published a magazine titled, *The Overcomer*. This was a Penn-Lewis idea in which Evan wrote an essay and she wrote the remainder of the issue."[29] It is my opinion that the magazine was just another tool of Penn-Lewis and her continued need to bring validity and popularity to her own work. It attacked early Pentecostal groups and listed their practices as satanic.

It was noticed in 1920 that Roberts was no longer contributing to the magazine, and he eventually moved to Brighton from where he wrote several booklets. The revival had passed, but it would not be forgotten, for the seeds of this revival were carried across the Atlantic Ocean and planted in fertile ground to manifest again in a new people.

ENDNOTES

1. Joseph Tracy, *The Great Awakening* (Carlisle, PA: The Banner of Truth and Trust, 1842), 214.

2. Winkey Pratney, *The Cane Ridge*, http://www.revivalfiretulsa.com/caneridgerevival.html.

3. Richard and Kathryn Riss, *Images of Revival* (Shippensburg, PA: Revival Press, 1997), 36.

4. Ibid., 37.

5. Robert M. Anderson, *Vision of the Disinherited* (MA: Hendrickson Publishers, 1979), 28, 29.

6. Charles Schmitt, *Floods Upon the Dry Ground* (Shippensburg, PA: Revival Press, 1998), 151.

7. http://www.geo.ed.ac.uk/scotgaz/people/famousfirst1143.html

8. http://www.biblewheel.com/History/C19_Holiness.asp

9. http://wesley.nnu.edu/wesleyan_theology/theojrnl/21-25/23-13.htm

10. Harold E. Raser, *Phoebe Palmer, Her Life and Thought* (Leiston: The Edwin Mellen Press, 1947), 79.

11. Richard Wheatley, *The Life and Letters of Mrs. Phoebe Palmer* (Garland Publishing, Inc., 1984), 640.

12. http://www.aaregistry.com/african_american_history/35/Amanda_Smith_missionary_with_a_quest

13. Robert Anderson , *Vision of the Disinherited* (Peabody, MA: Hendrickson 1979).

14. http://www.webedelic.com/church/penthisf.htm .

15. Gordon Lindsay, *John Alexander Dowie, A Christ for The Nations*, No copyright.

16. Roberts Liardon, *God's Generals* (New Kensington, PA: Whittaker House, 1996), 21.

17. Liardon, *God's Generals*, 41.

18. Anderson, *Visions of the Disinherited*, 128, 129.

19. Liardon, *God's Generals*, 51.

20. Maria Woodworth-Etter, *Signs and Wonder* (Chicago, 1916), 48.

21. Liardon, *God's Generals*, 72.

22. www.cogic.org/history.htm

23. R.B. Jones, *Rent Heavens* (Ashville, NC: Revival Literature, no copyright date), 47.

24. Liardon, *God's Generals*, 84.

25. Anderson, *Vision of the Disinherited*, 44.

26. Jones, *Rent Heavens*, 42.

27. Winkie Pratney, *Revival—Its Principles and Personalities* (Lafayette, LA: Huntington House),1994, 153.

28. Liardon, *God's Generals*, 100.

29. Liardon, *God's Generals*, 110.

Chapter Three

CHARLES PARHAM— THE FATHER OF PENTECOST

WHILE William Seymour was the catalyst of the modern-day Pentecostal movement, Charles Parham is known as the father of the movement. It was Charles Parham who first created the little fire that William Seymour would later stir into a blaze. Parham, the teacher, was the beginning of the experience and theology of Pentecost, and Seymour, the student, was the outburst and spread of Pentecost. Parham and Seymour were both children of the Holiness movement and would mature under the influence of the Pentecostal experience. They both longed for a resurrection of the primitive church with all its power and glory.

In addition, the Pentecostal movement was birthed in racial unity—Parham was white and Seymour was black; yet the movement would eventually fragment into racial prejudice and division.

THE EARLY DAYS

Understanding the religious atmosphere in the state of Kansas during those days will help us understand how fresh spiritual experiences became the perfect road to the recovery of lost dreams. Already Kansans had seen their share of religious prophets who were the forerunners of the moral majority. From John Brown's abolitionist crusades to Carrie

A. Nation's saloon-wrecking campaign, the state was producing a religious moral fervor. But this moral majority seemed destined to failure as many others in Kansas found other ways to get their tobacco and alcohol. The people were beginning to understand that the moral majority was a failed policy and that unless hearts were changed, the ways of man would not be changed.

Charles Parham was born on June 4, 1873, in Muscatine, Iowa, and shortly after his birth, the family moved to Cheney, Kansas. Parham was born a "sick and weakly" child and suffered a great deal throughout his childhood. "...early childhood was not easy for young Parham. At six months of age, he was stricken with a fever that left him bedridden. For the first five years of his life, he was plagued with dramatic spasms, and his forehead swelled making his head abnormally large."[1] At the age of 9, he began a battle with rheumatism that would leave him virtually tied up in a knot. Following that illness, he suffered with an attack of tapeworm. Parham was convinced later in life that the strong medicines he was forced to take as a child made him dwarfed in size. Because of these physical battles, he spent his earliest days under the constant supervision of his mother. Then in December 1885, his mother died during childbirth.

A FLASH FROM HEAVEN

In 1886, at the age of 13, Parham was converted when he stood up at a revival meeting and committed his life to God. But it was on the way home when the real conversion took place. Feeling a deep sense of conviction on the ride home, he started singing a Gospel hymn in order to assuage his sense of guilt. Reaching the third verse his experience reached a pinnacle as he continued to sing with his face lifted up to Heaven. Then it happened, as described in his own words:

> There flashed from the Heaven, a light above the brightness
> of the sun; like a stroke of lightning it penetrated, thrilling
> every tissue and fibre of our being; knowing by experimental

knowledge what Peter knew of old that He was the Christ, the Son of the living God.[2]

Parham became a Sunday school teacher in the local Methodist Church and by the age of 15 had held his own evangelistic meetings. At 16 he entered Southwestern Kansas College, a Methodist college in Winfield, Kansas, but because of the negative attitude of the scholarly folk around him toward preachers, Parham lost a bit of his passion for the ministry. He had suffered from so many diseases as a child; consequently, he decided to pursue a medical career. Ultimately, he would become a healer of men; but it would not be through the power of medicine but by the power of God.

While at school, he faced another physical battle. A physician who visited him, as his body was burning up with a severe fever and under an overdose of morphine, predicted his imminent death. For months he suffered, yet the suffering seemed to resurrect within him a new spiritual passion. So he cried out to God, "If you will let me go somewhere, someplace, where I wouldn't have to take collections or beg for a living, I will preach."[3] Not knowing how else to pray, he started reciting the Lord's Prayer; and when he came to "Thy Kingdom come, Thy will be done on earth as it is in heaven," he cried out, "If Thy will be done in me, I shall be made whole."

Under an old oak tree on the college lawn, he renewed his vow to preach the Gospel and promised to quit college if God would heal him. "Crawling under a tree, Parham began to pray, and God immediately sent a 'mighty electric current' through his ankles making them whole."[4]

He was healed, and he kept his promise to God. During May 1892, he held evangelistic meetings at the Pleasant-Valley School House near Tonganoxie, Kansas. While there, he was befriended by the Thistlethwaite, a Quaker family. Then at the annual meeting of the Southwest Kansas Conference in March 1893, he was licensed by the Methodist to preach. The following June he became pastor of the

Methodist church in Eudora, Kansas, just outside of Lawrence. He entered the pastorate with great enthusiasm, continuing his thrust for evangelism and fulfilling his pastoral roles.

I Left Denominationalism Forever

Earlier picture of Charles Parham
(Used by permission, Flower Pentecostal Heritage Center)

Parham was always thinking outside the religious box of his time, and it was inevitable that this freedom would eventually get him in trouble. By 1894, Parham's theology had become controversial within the Methodist conference. He embraced a form of "annihilation of the wicked"—a belief that the wicked would not have eternal life but would be annihilated and only the righteous would live forever. He also embraced the Holiness doctrine. And in an attempt to deemphasize denominational affiliation, he actively preached in non-Methodist circles, and he encouraged listeners to join other churches—or none at all.

"While listening to the presiding bishop ordain the new Conference members in 1895, he reportedly was 'horror-struck at the thought that the candidates were not left free to preach by direct inspiration.' He immediately surrendered his local preacher's license and severed all connections with the denomination."[5] Asserting that he could no longer accept salary raised by "suppers and worldly entertainment," Parham was tired and frustrated by the impositions of the denomination and also by the fact that he had experienced so little spiritual fruit while at Eudora.

> Finding the confines of a pastorate, and feeling the narrowness of sectarian churchism, I was often in conflict with the higher authorities, which eventually resulted in open rupture; and I left denominationalism forever, though suffering bitter persecution at the hands of the church...Oh, the narrowness of many who call themselves the Lord's own.[6]

Parham obeyed the call to enter the evangelistic fields and preached in Holiness churches wherever a door would open. He kept his friendship with the Thistlewaites and on New Year's Eve 1896 was married to Sarah, one of their daughters. After the traditional Quaker wedding they did not go on a traditional honeymoon; they commenced an evangelistic tour through Kansas and Missouri.[7]

LIVE OR DIE

In September 1897, Charles faced another medical crisis. He fell ill with a severe heart disease. It seemed that no matter what medicine he used or how much, it did not work. At the same time his newly born son, Claude, also came down with a severe fever.

While struggling with this sickness, he was called to pray for another sick man; and as he was praying, the Scripture, "Physician, heal thyself," came to his spirit. How could he pray for the sick when he was still suffering? At that moment, he prayed for himself, then threw away his medicine, gave up doctors, and cancelled his insurance policy. Not long after, both he and his son were healed.

Right after this experience, he received news that two of his closest friends had died. Consumed with grief, he hurried to their graves. That day marked a change in his life and ministry.

"As I knelt between the graves of my two loved friends, who might have lived if I had but told them of the power of Christ to heal, I made a vow that 'Live or Die' I would preach this Gospel of the healing."[8]

BETHEL—A PLACE OF HEALING

This powerful experience caused him to make a shift in his ministry, and from that point forward, he began to focus on divine healing. He determined that his ministry would be a ministry of salvation from both sin and sickness. In 1898, Parham packed his bags and took his family to Ottawa, Kansas, bought the old Salvation Army building, and started preaching the Gospel of salvation and healing. He was met with immediate success as many were being healed. This was the beginning of a rising notoriety, and later in the year, he moved his family to Topeka and rented a building at the corner of Fourth and Jackson Streets in the downtown area. The Bethel Healing Home, as he called it, would now become the center of Parham's burgeoning ministry.

This new place was a combination rest home and Bible school, where people were admitted on a "faith basis." Here in this spiritual environment, they could expose themselves to the healing power of God, and students would be taught the ways of the Spirit. According to his wife, Parham's teachings at this time were: "Salvation, Healing, Sanctification, the Second coming of Christ, and the Baptism of the Holy Spirit, although he had not then received the evidence of speaking in other tongues."[9]

Parham was focused on the healing message. His opposition to medicine was strongly built on a skepticism of the effectiveness of medicine at that time as well as a confidence that it was God's will to heal all who would come to Him in faith. Parham saw a parallel between God's power to deliver one from sin and His power to heal one from sickness. In desperation he once cried out, "Friends, we will never get rid of the devil until we quit this everlasting nursing of our diseases."[10] Parham estimated that half of all diseases were psychosomatic and recommended that once people threw back their shoulders and faced the world with a smile and cheerful disposition, the afflictions would disappear.

THE APOSTOLIC FAITH

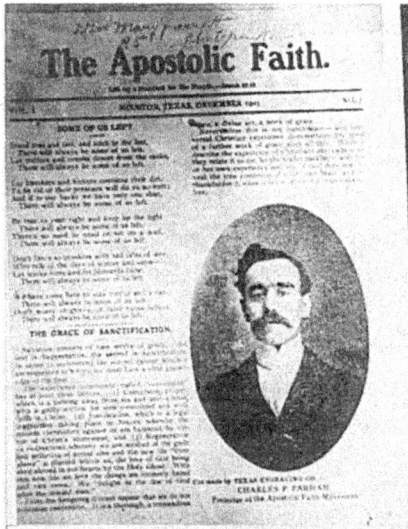

Issue No. 7 of The Apostolic Faith newsletter
(Used by permission, Flower Pentecostal Heritage Center)

To publicize and coordinate the variety of religious services at Bethel, in March 1899, Parham started publishing a newsletter that he called *The Apostolic Faith*. Regular subscribers probably numbered only a few hundred in the beginning, but as many as 500 additional copies were distributed free with each issue. "...*The Apostolic Faith* was published bi-weekly, had a subscription rate at first (one dollar a year)...The newsletter published wonderful testimonies of healing and many of the sermons that were taught at Bethel."[11]

Staples, a local publisher who shared editorial responsibilities with Parham, wrote about the moral values of the newsletter:

> We want this paper to run for the glory of God, and intend that it shall be. We believe the great majority of papers and magazines of this day cannot be safely brought into the home, because of vileness, displayed in various ways. If you subscribe for the APOSSOLIC FAITH [sic] you need not be afraid to let your children read it. They will not find any tobacco advertisements in it, not anything that defiles. They will not find any vile or abominable jokes in it. If there are any they will be pure.[12]

A Growing Dissatisfaction and a New Beginning

Even though he was experiencing a measure of success, Parham had hoped to accomplish a lot more in Topeka, Kansas, and was consequently growing more and more disenchanted with his ministry. With increased pressures mounting around him, he again began to seek the Lord for new direction. He had been reading and admiring the works of A.B. Simpson and was especially impressed with the results of Dowie's healing campaigns.

In the meantime, a number of visitors to Topeka were relating to Parham about the Spirit in Holiness centers in the North and East. So, Parham decided to visit one of these centers in Durham, Maine, headed by Frank Sandford, who had become independent after leaving the Free Baptist group. Leaving the work in the hands of a couple of Holiness preachers, he headed for Maine. On the way he also visited Dowie's work in Chicago, Malone's work in Cincinnati, and A.B. Simpson's work in Nyack, New York.

Parham ended up staying for six weeks at Shiloh in Durham, Maine where he was deeply impressed with the message of the Holy Spirit being taught. He had long been seeking a fresh revelation concerning the Baptism of the Spirit, and while there he came to accept their position that the Baptism of the Spirit was for deeply consecrated believers and that it would result in a world evangelism effort of renewed spiritual power.

Parham eagerly returned home, refreshed and renewed with an even deeper hunger. The following words contain the seeds of the truths that Parham discovered and revealed:

> I returned home fully convinced that while many had obtained real experiences in sanctification and the anointing that abideth, there still remained a great outpouring of power for the Christians who were close to this age.[13]

But when he arrived home, much to his surprise, he found that the two Holiness preachers had literally taken over his work and had locked him out. So as not to create an opportunity for the devil to create a scandal, Parham sought the Lord for a new place for his work. At that time, because of the tremendous success at Bethel, many were urging him to open a Bible school. So, Parham shut himself away for fasting and prayer, and then in October 1900, through the help of agents of the American Bible Society, he obtained an unfinished mansion on the outskirts of Topeka. A new beginning was ahead. It was there that he opened his Bible school built on the success he had seen in Maine.

STONE'S FOLLY

Parham was a brash, 27-year-old spiritually zealous young man when he established Bethel Bible College, located two miles outside Topeka's business section, in mid-October 1900. The mansion that he purchased in a sparsely settled residential district was called Stone's Folly and was patterned after an English castle. "It was a jumble of red brick, white stone, balustrades, ornate cornices, stained glass windows, and doors, with cupolas, tall chimneys, and a soaring observatory. Each of the completed rooms was finished in paneling of different exotic woods."[14] The 40 by 75-foot structure stood 60 feet tall. But the builder ran out of money before the structure could be completed. However, Stone's Folly was large enough to house Parham's new ministry.

Stone's Folly, where the fire first fell

Parham's school opened on October 15, 1900 with about 36 students, most of whom had been ministers from other denominations in the area and shared with Parham his intense desire for a new Pentecostal blessing.

"In imitation of Sandord's Shiloh techniques, the Bethel school was operated 'on faith,' (trusting God for all of their finances) the Bible was the only textbook, a 'prayer chain' in three-hour shifts was maintained in one of the tower rooms, several rooms were set aside for a healing home, and much time was given to fasting and prayer."[15]

A HOLY SPIRIT MEETING, A HALO,
AND SUPERNATURAL POWER

Parham taught extemporaneously, verse by verse, from the Scriptures; and the students learned as they took copious notes of everything Parham was teaching. During the days the students went door-to-door witnessing, and in the evenings they held services at the mansion. When they got to the Book of Acts, Parham gave his students an assignment. They were to diligently search for the evidence of Spirit baptism as seen in Acts and then report on what they had found. It is clear that Parham had probably already arrived at the conclusion that the gift of tongues was the evidence of one having received the gift of the Spirit, but he wanted his students to also reach that conclusion. Parham left town for a meeting in Kansas, and when he returned to Stone's Folly, he was eager to see the results of the assignment. He listened intently to the reports of the students. Their conclusion was that every recipient of the baptism of the Spirit spoke in tongues. This discovery created a spiritual atmosphere ripe for an encounter with God.

Anticipation now filled the house as 75 people gathered together for the evening Watch Night service on January 1, 1901. One of the students in the meeting was 30-year-old Agnes N. Ozman. Ozman had attended T.C. Horton's Bible school in Minnesota and A.B. Simpson's Nyack institute, visited Dowie's work in Chicago, and had worked from time to time during the previous 12 years. Ozman had been on a long spiritual odyssey and was hungry for spiritual power. Prior to this meeting, Ozman mentioned that she had spoken a couple of words in another language but was still spiritually hungry for a full experience in the Holy Spirit.[16]

That evening, during the service, Ozman went up to Parham and asked him if he would lay hands on her so that she would receive the Spirit baptism. At Ozman's persistence and although Parham himself had not spoken in tongues, he laid hands on the student. Parham would later record his observations as to what happened next.

I had scarcely repeated three dozen sentences when a glory fell upon her, a halo seemed to surround her head and face, and she began speaking in the Chinese language, and was unable to speak in English for three days.[17]

TONGUES OF FIRE

Agnes Oxman, first woman recorded to have spoken in tongues
(Used by permission, Flower Pentecostal Heritage Center)

At the urging of Ozman, for two days and three nights, the students turned their dormitory into a prayer room and sought the power of the Spirit. On the evening of January 3, while Parham was preaching at a free Methodist church in Topeka, about the wonderful events at Stone's Folly, the Spirit fell on the students at the Bethel school. When Parham arrived back at the school, a student met him at the door and led him to the Prayer Room. Inside he encountered 12 students who were sitting, standing, kneeling, and all speaking in tongues.

Overwhelmed by what he saw, Parham fell to his knees and started praying and praising God. While he was praying, he distinctly heard God tell him that he was to proclaim this Holy Spirit baptism and this mighty outpouring. Counting the cost, Parham said that he would obey. At that moment, he was also filled with the Holy Spirit and began to speak in other tongues. Here is how Parham described the experience in his own words: Right then and there came a slight twist in my throat, a glory fell over me and I began to worship God in a Swedish tongue, which later changed to other languages and continued....[18]

Charles Parham (in center) with staff and students
(Used by permission, Flower Pentecostal Heritage Center)

Although there were already those who had spoken in tongues before the events at Stone's Folly, this was the first time that tongues was linked as the evidence of being baptized in the Holy Spirit. This event in Topeka became the watershed of the Pentecostal movement. In actuality, Parham pieced together the theological puzzle of Pentecostalism during the fall of 1900, but it was during the Topeka Outpouring that his theology would become an experience. Parham was convinced that this fresh outpouring of the Holy Spirit would lead to world evangelism, and missions would remain a focus of Parham's preaching till the very end.

TRAGEDY AND PERSECUTION STRIKES AGAIN

As it was with the early disciples who experienced the first Pentecostal outpouring, so it would be with Parham. It seems there are those within the religious system who are always ready to oppose and abuse any fresh move of God.

About half the students had received the Holy Spirit and had spoken in tongues, but there were a few others who remained disgruntled. One of those students was S.J. Riggins, who had already had a run-in with some of the students. Riggins did not speak in tongues and left the school telling everyone that it was fake, which only served to give the school and Parham more notoriety as the *Topeka State Journal* and other newspapers were now picking up the story. Parham remained inspired and motivated to take on the battle of declaring the truth of his new revelation of the Holy Spirit.

Unfortunately, tragedy struck when their youngest child, Charles, died in March 1901. This heartbreaking event combined with the persecution aimed at them served to intensify their grief. It would have been tempting for any mortal person to simply give up, but Parham was built from a different character than the average person. He found a new strength by keeping his heart tender before the Lord and refusing to allow bitterness to ruin him.

Then, to make matters worse, in the fall of 1901, the Bible school in Topeka was sold out from under him. Without a home, Parham moved his family to Kansas City. The group who went with him secured a small building at 1675 Madison Avenue in downtown Kansas City and began holding services. It was at this time that Parham began to travel more extensively preaching the message of the Holy Spirit baptism; and then in January 1902, he published his first book, *Kol Kare Bomidbar* (Hebrew meaning: A Voice Crying in the Wilderness). The book was filled with sermons on salvation, healing, and sanctification and marked the first publication of a book about Pentecostal theology by a Pentecostal.

MANY CAME TO SCOFF BUT REMAINED TO PRAY

Parham, the rejected prophet, was looking for a place to land. He had spent a year and a half in Lawrence, Kansas, without must success, and in the fall of 1903 he again moved his family, this time to Galena, Kansas, erecting a large tent and conducting the first Pentecostal camp meeting. The tent could hold 2,000 people but still proved to be too small, so a building was located as winter set in. "Huge numbers poured into Galena from surrounding towns when strong manifestations of the Spirit occurred and hundreds were miraculously saved."[19] One newspaper reported that 500 were converted, about 250 were baptized in the icy waters of the Spring River, and many were baptized in the Spirit. But the thing that caught people's attention was the healings. By Thanksgiving 1904, Parham was enjoying the most sustained meeting of his career, yet he was always careful to deflect attention from himself reminding the people that he was not the healer and that their healing was from God. Over 800 new converts joined his alliance, and over 1,000 people claimed healing. On New Year's Eve, the revival attracted close to 2,500 eager worshipers. It was evident that the Pentecostal experience was gaining a foothold.

Then in 1905, Parham accepted an invitation for a three-week vacation in Orchard, Texas, just outside of Houston. Once there, he experienced a rapid recovery from an illness, sparked by the enthusiasm in the town. Preaching his first sermon on Easter Sunday, Parham quickly reaped a wonderful harvest as many were saved. In addition, while he was ministering in Orchard, Parham was inspired to begin holding "Rally Days." He and his team would march down the streets dressed in the clothes of Bible days, and the first Rally Day was planned to take place in Houston, Texas.

HOUSTON—BIBLE SCHOOL WITH A FAMOUS STUDENT

Parham and 25 workers held the first Rally Day meeting in Houston at the Bryn Hall. One of the big attractions was Parham's "Holy Land" array of 15 Palestinian robes that depicted the lifestyle of the social classes of Bible times. He also used large, colorful flags and banners. "Bearing inscriptions of 'unity' and 'victory,' the Pentecostal robe-clad army marched down the street proclaiming a revolution of apostolic Christianity."[20] W. Faye Carothers, who had learned of Parham's efforts, joined him in the crusade in Houston. Eventually, Carothers would become Parham's right-hand man, and his church in Brunner became the Texas headquarters for the Apostolic Faith Movement. In December 1905, Parham opened a Bible school in Houston and moved the printing of his newspaper to Houston. The school was operated on the same principles as the Bethel school in Topeka, Kansas. The students were required to live by faith and trust God for their financial needs, pooling all resources together in order to live.

Charles Parham and team with display of flags and banners
(Used by permission, Flower Pentecostal Heritage Center)

Among the most significant things that happened in the Bible school was the meeting between Charles Parham and William J. Seymour. While in Houston, Seymour visited an African-American mission and heard someone speak in tongues. It is very likely that it was Lucy Farrow who often frequented the African-American Holiness missions with Parham. Lucy Farrow was the black governess in Parham's home, and she is quite likely the link between Parham and Seymour.

The Jim Crow laws of the day prevented blacks and whites from congregating together; therefore, there were no blacks allowed in the school. Seymour, though, showed up at Parham's school asking for entrance. Because of the policy of segregation, Parham was reluctant, but sensing Seymour's great spiritual hunger, he eventually allowed him to attend. Parham, also sensitive to the local Jim Crow laws, admitted Seymour to the Bible school but did not allow him to sit in the classroom with the white students. Consequently, Seymour sat in an adjoining room where, through an open door, he absorbed the daily teachings on the Holy Spirit baptism.

One day in January 1906, Seymour went to Parham to discuss an invitation that had been sent to him to preach in Los Angeles. Parham tried to convince him to stay, but once again, the zealous Seymour won. From their general treasury, Parham gave Seymour the money for the train trip, and then in a momentous act, he laid hands on the kneeling Seymour and sent him on his way. Little did they know at that time that Seymour's trip would strike a match and set off a new blaze of Pentecostal fire.

RACE ISSUE

In the early days in Houston, Parham would often preach in the black missions with Seymour; consequently, there were several black ministers who joined his movement. But as Parham got older, his racial philosophy unfortunately became more entrenched in the racial prejudice of his day. Carothers was not fond of Parham's openness and outlined his own racial convictions. Carothers' idea was that the Pentecostal revival should spread from white to white and black to black. Pentecost had come, but it had not yet broken the racial divide. Parham fluctuated between Carothers' social segregation and Dowie's open racial policy. In fact, Dowie desired to see a country where there was full racial equality. In an era when racial segregation was the law of the land, Dowie insisted on integration in his meetings and preached against the scourge of racial inequality.[21]

In either case, Parham was neither a racial reformer nor a champion of white supremacy; rather, he occupied a paternalistic middle ground typical of many, if not most, white ministers from the Midwest. But by the mid-1920s Parham was writing articles for the anti-Semitic, anti-Catholic, and racist periodical of Gerald Winrod. On one occasion he referred to the Klansmen as "those splendid men."[22]

PARHAM GOES TO ZION

By the summer of 1906, Parham had a movement of roughly 8,000 to 10,000 people and had started a Pentecostal fire that would never burn out. Of the total number of people who were part of the movement, Azusa Street encompassed no more than 800 to 1000, or one tenth of the movement in August 1906.

Since the initial, poor reception following the Topeka outbreak in January 1901, Parham had rebounded with a steady string of successful revival ventures. He showed his concern over the increased numbers by providing, in early 1906, a form for converting the movement into a more structured organization. Parham appointed his sister-in-law, Lilian Thistlethwaite, as General Secretary of the Apostolic Faith Movement. He personally retained the title, Projector of the Apostolic Faith, and assumed overseership of the general organization.

Beginning in May 1906, all evangelists and full-time workers received official credentials signed by Projector Parham and their respective state directors. Seymour wrote State Director Carothers and also received his credentials in July.

In addition, Dowie's decline created a vacuum among his own members, which offered Parham an unprecedented opportunity to advance the Apostolic Faith. With contacts around the world that numbered over 25,000, success in Zion could mean an almost instant start of the global Pentecostal revival.

Parham felt by God that he was to hold a rally in Zion City, Illinois. When he arrived, he found the ministry in great turmoil. Dowie had been discredited, and there was great discouragement among the Zion community. Soon Parham began cottage meetings in some of the best homes in the city. But the opposition was too great for Parham. The negative blitz from the secular media was creating great distraction as they sought to discredit Parham. Even Dowie, himself, spoke out against Parham and his message. Wilbur Voliva, who had taken over after the demise of Dowie, encouraged Parham to leave. In the face of opposition and with the news of the revival that hit Azusa, Parham packed his bags and headed for Los Angeles.

PARHAM AT AZUSA

No one knows what exactly Parham expected to see when he arrived in Los Angeles, even though he had previously seen reports from the newspapers that described the fanaticism of the revival. When Parham finally arrived in Los Angeles, he was careful to distance himself from the fanaticism and even accused outside sources of infiltrating the work at Azusa.

To clearly disassociate himself with the disturbing reports, he offered a scathing denunciation of fanatical "Holy Rollers" and explained the differences between them and his own followers. "We have no sympathy with nor do we countenance the gymnastic contortions of the Holy Rollers, who throw fits, perform somersaults, roll and kick in the straw or dust or upon the floor of the meeting house."[23]

When Parham arrived at Azusa, he entered an environment that appeared to be totally out of control and somewhat resistant to his spiritual leadership. In one of his newspapers, he mentioned that fanaticism will always lead to spiritual pride and subsequently accused Seymour of becoming "possessed with a spirit of leadership."

Many Azusa worshipers rejected the idea that an "outsider" could suddenly arrive and "correct" their revival pattern. Parham was also offended by the interracial nature of the meetings and graphically explained to his audiences that the "sin" of intermarriage in the days of Noah had been the chief cause of the Flood.[24]

Parham had hoped to bring correction and direction to this work of God, but after only two or three messages, he was rejected and locked out of the Azusa meetings. After remaining a little longer in Los Angeles, he returned to Zion in December 1906. In an effort to resurrect a work there, he pitched a tent in a large open lot, but the opposition was horrific, so he left for a prolonged ministry in Canada and New England. Unable to sustain the criticism and persecution, Mrs. Parham decided to take her children back to Kansas.

A FALLEN STAR

This was the beginning of the end. Parham's ministry had already reached its apex and now was declining. Because of his insistence in building a work in Chicago, he had created very powerful enemies including Wilbur Voliva, who was now head of Zion City. Rumors of immorality began circulating as early as January 1907. Local papers suggested that Parham's sudden departure on a northeastern tour was prompted by the arrival of "mysterious men, said to be detectives, who were ready to arrest him on some equally mysterious charge."[25]

The nature of the rumors became public when the charges appeared in the *San Antonio Light* on July 20, 1907. Officially, Parham was charged with homosexuality, but Parham quickly retaliated announcing that he was the victim of an elaborate frame devised by his arch nemesis, Wilbur Voliva.

"C.F. Parham...about 40 years old, and J.J. Jourdan, 22 years old, were arrested about noon today upon an affidavit made before Justice of the Peace Ben S. Fisk, charging the commission of an unnatural offense..."[26]

Poster advertising special meetings with Charles Parham
(Used by permission, Flower Pentecostal Heritage Center)

After making a payment of $1,000, they were both released. Conspicuously silent in the days after the arrest was J.J. Jourdan, Parham's codefendant. But the case was never called, and the prosecuting attorney declared that there was not enough evidence to bring a conviction. Shortly thereafter, the news died down, at least in the secular press. In the Christian community, this would not be the case. Voliva, through his newspaper, *The Zion Herald,* perpetuated and enhanced the news out of San Antonio. The religious henchmen had done their job well, and it seemed that Parham would not easily remove the noose they had prepared for him.

Parham's alleged homosexuality was a source of immense embarrassment for him and his wife, and eventually his good friend, W. Faye Carothers, would break away from the organization. Yet even in the face of such adversity, the Apostolic Faith doctrine continued to spread, and by the fall of 1908, there were more than 60 different Pentecostal missions scattered throughout the United States.

During the years that followed, Parham continued to travel, preaching wherever there was an open door. Unfortunately, the past followed him, but he persevered in his commitment to proclaim the gospel of healing and the baptism of the Holy Spirit.

In April 1916, he changed the name of his monthly publication from *The Apostolic Faith* to *The Everlasting Gospel* and geared the articles toward the war and its relationship to biblical prophecy. In 1919, he published his second book, also titled, *The Everlasting Gospel.*

Parham continued to draw occasional crowds of several thousand in small towns and cities where he gave stock sermons and lectures and presented a variety hour of gospel music entertainment. In the winter of 1924, Parham held meetings in Oregon and Washington, and it was while Parham was speaking at John G. Lake's church that Gordon Lindsay, founder of Christ for the Nations, found salvation.

By August 1928, Parham had grown tired, and his time on this earth was coming to an end. To one of his friends he wrote:

"I am living on the edge of glory land these days and it's all so real on the other side of the curtain that I feel mightily tempted to cross over."[27]

On the last day of his time on earth, Parham was heard saying, "Peace, peace, like a river. That is what I have been thinking all day." On January 29, 1929, at the age of 56, Charles F. Parham died.

But before he died, his ministry contributed to over two million conversions. His crowds often exceeded 7,000, and it was Parham who popularized the message of Pentecost and prepared the way for all that happened at Azusa. The father was now to give way to the catalyst of Pentecost.

ENDNOTES

1. James Goff, *Fields White Unto Harvest*, 26.

2. Liardon, *God's Generals*, 112.

3. Mrs. Charles Parham, *The Life of Charles F. Parham* (Birmingham, AL: Commercial Printing Co., 1930), 6-9.

4. Anderson, *Fields White Unto Harvest*, 36.

5. Liardon, *God's Generals*, 113.

6. Anderson, *Vision of the Disinherited*, 49.

7. Charles Parham, *The Life of Charles F. Parham*, 33.

8. Anderson, *Vision of the Disinherited*, 50.

9. Goff, *Fields White Unto Harvest*, 37 (From a pamphlet written by Parham on Divine Healing).

10. Liardon, *God's Generals*, 116.

11. Goff, *Fields White Unto Harvest* (first issue of *The Apostolic Faith* newsletter), 46.

12. Mrs. Charles Parham, *The Life of Charles Parham*, 48.

13. Anderson, *Vision of the Disinherited*, 51.

14. Ibid., 51.

15. Anderson, *Vision of the Disinherited* (quoted from *Life of Charles Parham* written by Sarah Parham), 56.

16. Liardon, *God's Generals*, 119.

17. Ibid., 120.

18. Ibid., 123.

19. Goff, *Fields White Unto Harvest*, 97.

20. Ibid., 110.

21. Anderson, *Vision of the Disinherited*, 190.

22. Goff, *Fields White Unto Harvest*, 128.

23. Liardon, *God's Generals*, 128.

24. Goff, *Fields White Unto Harvest*, 131.

25. Liardon, *God's Generals*, 129.

26. Goff, *Fields White Unto Harvest*, 136.

27. Liardon, *God's Generals*, 132.

Chapter Four

WILLIAM SEYMOUR—
THE CATALYST OF PENTECOST

T HE Protestant reformation began with Martin Luther in Wittenburg, Germany, in a broken-down building in the midst of the public square—a humble beginning for a revival that would shake the world. D'Aubigne described that place[1]:

Martin Luther nailing the 95 theses to the Wittenburg door

In the middle of the square at Wittenberg stood an ancient wooden chapel, thirty feet long and twenty feet wide, whose walls, propped up on all sides, were falling into ruin. An old pulpit made of planks, and three feet high, received the preacher. It was in this wretched place that the preaching of the Reformation began. It was God's will that that which was to restore His glory should have the humblest surroundings. It was in this wretched enclosure that God willed, so to speak, that His well-beloved Son should be born a second time. Among those thousands of cathedrals and parish churches with which the world is filled, there was not one at that time which God chose for the glorious preaching of eternal life.

Similarly, a few hundred years later on a dead-end street in the middle of the industrial section of Los Angeles, California, the beginning of the Pentecostal movement would begin in a humble, former Methodist church building at 312 Azusa Street. In that modest building, an unassuming group of racially mixed folk who were hungry for the presence of God would experience the Pentecostal fire falling upon them. The leader was not a theologian with a compelling presence or commanding speech. He was a humble, one-eyed black man with a light beard and a face scarred by smallpox who came from Houston, Texas, with the Pentecostal message burning in his heart.

Azusa Street Mission, April 1906
(Used by permission, Flower Pentecostal Heritage Center)

Ku Klux Klan, Jim Crow, and the Birth of a Preacher

William J. Seymour was born on May 2, 1870, in Centerville, Louisiana. His parents, Simon and Phyllis, were freed from slavery only a few years earlier. Seymour was born in a time when racial prejudice was rampant. The Ku Klux Klan was visible in almost every community in the South, and the Jim Crow Law was in full force preventing the mixing of the races. Jim Crow was the name of the racial caste system that operated primarily, but not exclusively in Southern and border states, between 1877 and the mid-1960s. Jim Crow was more than a series of rigid anti-black laws; it was a way of life. Under Jim Crow, African-Americans were relegated to the status of second-class citizens. These heinous laws enforced separate use of water fountains, public bathhouses, and separate seating sections on public transport. The Jim Crow laws represented the legitimization of anti-black racism. Sadly, discrimination and segregation were also prevalent in the churches, and many Christian ministers and theologians taught that whites were the "chosen people," blacks were cursed to be servants, and God supported racial segregation. Many in those days did not believe that blacks even had a soul. The coming Pentecostal revival would eventually drive a stake into the heart of these detestable laws and beliefs.

Young Seymour "found his identity in Jesus Christ, believing that the Lord was the only liberator of mankind. He was a sensitive, high-spirited youth, and hungry for the truth of God's Word. It is said he experienced divine visions, and that early in life began to look for the return of Jesus Christ."[2] With no formal education, like many others in those times, he taught himself to read by constantly reading the Bible. He was christened in the Roman Catholic church and was probably raised in the Catholic church, although some believe that he was raised as a Baptist.

RESTLESS AND SEARCHING

There were few who were willing to leave their hometowns in those days, but Seymour, restless and a man on the move, left Louisiana in 1891 while he was still in his 20s. First, he went to Memphis, Tennessee where he worked as a porter in a barbershop and then as a driver for the Tennessee Paper Company. In 1893 he traveled up the Mississippi River and landed in St. Louis, Missouri where he worked as a bartender.[3]

Seymour arrived in Indianapolis, Indiana at the age of 25 and found work as a waiter in some of the city's finest restaurants. Not long after his arrival, Seymour joined the A.B. Simpson Chapel Methodist Episcopal Church. This branch of the Northern Methodists had a strong evangelistic outreach to all classes, which appealed greatly to Seymour. Their passion to reach out to all helped Seymour formulate his belief that there is no color line in the redemption of Christ.

In 1895 Seymour moved to Cincinnati, Ohio, where he continued to work as a waiter. While there he came into contact with holiness teachings through Martin Wells Knapp's God's Revivalist movement and Daniel S. Warner's Church of God Reformation movement, otherwise known as the Evening Light Saints. Believing that they were living in the twilight of human history, these Christians believed that the Spirit's outpouring would precede the rapture of the Church. These teachings deeply impressed the young Seymour."[4]

It was while he was with this group that he received his call to the ministry—a call he wrestled with. In the midst of the struggle, he contracted smallpox, which was usually fatal in that time. He survived three weeks of horrible suffering and was left with blindness in his left eye and severe facial scarring.[5] After his recovery, he immediately submitted to the call of God and was licensed and ordained as a minister by Evening Light Saints. Soon, he began traveling as an itinerant preacher.

By 1900, there were 30 black leaders in the group, and they strongly encouraged their ministers to work hand in hand.[6] The emphasis on unity again strengthened Seymour's resolve to see a united people serving the purposes of God.

Seymour left Cincinnati sometime in 1902, and there remains uncertainty regarding his whereabouts until he arrived in Houston, Texas, in 1905.

HOUSTON, PARHAM, AND GOING TO BIBLE SCHOOL

In the summer of 1905, the Houston newspapers included glowing terms about Charles Parham and his crusades in Bryn Hall in downtown Houston. At that time, Houston was a city of cultural variety, and people of all races were drawn to Parham's meetings. While attending the meetings, Lucy Farrow, an African-American believer, became friends with the Parham family and was soon offered the position of governess. Although she was pastor of a small Holiness church, she decided to return to Kansas with the Parhams when they left Texas. At that time, she had recently become friends with Seymour and asked him to pastor the Holiness church until she returned a couple of months later.[7]

When Mrs. Farrow returned, she could not wait to tell Seymour of her experiences in the Parham home. While she was with the Parhams, she was baptized in the Holy Spirit and spoke in tongues. Seymour was a bit reluctant to accept this "new doctrine" as he believed that he had already been baptized in the Spirit when he was sanctified in Cincinnati. However, after a time of searching the Scriptures and praying, his heart was changed. In a book written by Sarah Parham, *Life Of Charles F. Parham*, Parham says that the Lord revealed to Seymour that he had been mistaken in his doctrinal position, and as a result, he accepted the idea that the Holy Spirit baptism was a third work of grace.[8]

As mentioned previously, in 1905, Parham announced that he would open a Bible school in Houston that would be formed similar to the school in Topeka. It was a communal-type living arrangement in one house, where the students and the instructor spent days and nights together in praying and studying the Word in an informal fashion.[9]

When Seymour heard about the school, he begged Parham to let him attend. Parham, however, was reluctant because of the Jim Crow laws, but at the insistence of Mrs. Farrow, he finally relented. He would allow him to sit outside the window and listen, and on rainy days he could sit in the hallway where they would leave the classroom door open. And because of his race, Seymour was not allowed to "tarry" at the altar seeking the Holy Spirit with the other white students. Despite the impositions from Parham, Seymour was not deterred, and because of the intensity of his spiritual hunger, he did extremely well in school. "Later he would be able to recite Parham's teachings word for word."[10]

THE CALL TO LOS ANGELES

William Seymour
(Used by permission, Flower Pentecostal Heritage Center)

Undaunted in his spiritual pursuit, Seymour continued to preach and testify at the black missions in Houston, and it was at one of these missions that he met Neely Terry. "She told Seymour that in her home church in Los Angeles, a Black Baptist congregation, a certain Sister Hutchins had recently preached at a revival and sounded much like him."[11] When Terry returned to Los Angeles, she then told Julia Hutchins about Seymour's unusual and powerful preaching. Subsequently, Julia Hutchins sent a letter to Seymour requesting that he come and assist her in the work in LA.

Seymour described his call to Los Angeles in the first issue of *The Apostolic Faith* newspaper, the official voice of the Azusa revival:

It was the divine call that brought me from Houston, Texas, to Los Angeles. The Lord put it in the heart of one of the saints in Los Angeles to write to me that she felt the Lord would have me come over here and do a work, and I came, for I felt it was the leading of the Lord. The Lord sent the means, and I came to take charge of a mission on Santa Fe Street, and one night they locked the door against me, and afterwards got Bro. Roberts, the president of the Holiness Association, to come down and settle the doctrine of the baptism of the Holy Spirit, that it was simply sanctification. He came down and a good many Holiness preachers with him, and they stated that sanctifica- tion was the baptism of the Holy Spirit. But yet they did not have the evidence of the second chapter of Acts, for when the disciples were all filled with the Holy Ghost, they spoke in tongues as the Spirit gave utterance. After the president heard me speak of what the true baptism of the Holy Ghost was, he said he wanted it too, and told me when I had received it to let him know. So I received it and let him know. The beginning of the Pentecost started in a cottage prayer meeting at 214 Bonnie Brae. (Apostolic Faith Vol.1, No. 1.)

When Seymour received the invitation to Los Angeles, he discussed it with Parham, who was not in favor of him leaving. Parham tried to convince him to stay until he received the Holy Spirit. He also wanted him to remain and work among the blacks in the city. "But once again Seymour won out, and Parham gave him railroad fare out of the common treasury. With prayer and the laying on of hands, Seymour was dispatched from Houston to Los Angeles sometime in January, 1906."[12]

214 NORTH BONNIE BRAE STREET

Many evangelists had been stirring the hungry hearts in Southern California for a number of years, and there was already evidence of a spiritual stirring in Los Angeles before Seymour arrived. Many groups were engaged in intense prayer, door-to-door witnessing, and waiting for the coming revival that they longed to see. Los Angeles, a melting pot of various ethnic groups, was the fastest growing city from 1880-1910; and blacks, Orientals, and Mexicans accounted for 5.6 percent of the population. By 1906, there were over 100 churches preaching the "full gospel" in the city.[13]

One particular group, the First Baptist Church of Los Angeles, was waiting for the return of their pastor, Rev. Joseph Smale. He had been on a three-week trip to Wales to sit under the teachings of the great Welsh revivalist, Evan Roberts. Smale was on fire for God and was hoping to bring the same revival that had visited Wales, home with him to Los Angeles.[14]

Another evangelist and developing journalist joined the Smale church—his name was Frank Bartleman. Bartleman was born in Carversville, Pennsylvania in 1871. He was saved in 1893 and accepted the call to preach. He preached as a Baptist, a Methodist, a cadet in the Salvation Army, and then as a Holiness preacher. At one time, while he was in Chicago, he was blessed to hear D.L. Moody preach.

Frank Bartleman
(Used by permission, Flower Pentecostal Heritage Center)

In 1905, he arrived with his family in Los Angeles, and while there, he corresponded with Welsh revivalist Evan Roberts about his passion for revival to come to California. Bartleman stated that it was these letters that encouraged him to believe that a revival would come.

Shortly after Seymour's arrival in Los Angeles, he preached his first sermon at Sister Hutchin's church on Santa Fe Avenue. His theology on the Holy Spirit would clash with hers because that church believed that they had already been sanctified and received the Holy Spirit. The clash came to a head when he was finally locked out of the church. Sister Hutchin would not allow his "extreme" form of teaching to take place in her church. Consequently, Seymour was left without any money or a place to stay. Fortunately, a family of the church, the Lees, opened their home to Seymour, and he remained there continuing in prayer and fasting and looking for God's direction.

He soon began organizing prayer meetings in the homes of black friends for those who were hungry to hear to his message. Then Mr. and Mrs. Richard Asberry invited him to stay in their home on North

Bonnie Brae Street. Seymour accepted, and they started holding meetings in their home in February 1906. Seymour made a strong pitch to the group to invite Lucy Farrow to come join the group. Consequently, money was collected to bring Miss Farrow, and when she arrived, Seymour called for ten days of prayer and fasting. During that time, Edward Lee, a janitor employed at the First National Bank, asked Seymour to come pray for him because of his ailing health. Seymour arrived, anointed him with oil, and he was healed. Then Lee asked him to pray for the baptism of the Holy Spirit. Even though Seymour had not personally received the experience, he prayed for Lee, and Lee immediately began speaking in tongues. They couldn't wait to get to the meeting that night.

214 Bonnie Brae Street
(Used by permission, Flower Pentecostal Heritage Center)

When they arrived at the Asberry Home on Bonnie Brae Street, every room was packed with people. Many were already praying. Seymour took charge of the meeting, leading the group in songs, testimonies, and more prayer. Then, he began to tell the story of Mr. Lee's healing and his infilling of the Holy Spirit. As soon as Seymour finished, Lee raised his hands and began to speak in tongues. The entire group dropped to their knees as they worshiped God and cried out for the baptism. Then, six or seven people lifted their voices and began to speak in another tongue. Jenny Evans Moore, who would later marry Seymour, fell to her knees from the piano bench as one of the first to speak in tongues.[15]

For three days they celebrated "early Pentecost restored." The news spread quickly bringing crowds that would fill the Asberry's house and the yard surrounding their home. It is said that the Asberry's front porch became the pulpit, and the street the pews, as Seymour would address the people from this home.

It was on the third night that Seymour would finally experience his own encounter with the Holy Spirit. Late on the evening of April 12, 1906, after many had already left the meeting, the long awaited gift finally came to the man who had been preaching of this gift for so many others.

THE MOVE TO AZUSA STREET

Azusa Street Mission, April 1906
(Used by permission, Flower Pentecostal Heritage Center)

There was no keeping the crowds away, and because of the loud prayers that disturbed the neighbors and the increasing number of people cramped into small quarters, there became an urgent need to find a larger building at a different location. Seymour's friends quickly located a vacant, two-story, whitewashed, wooden frame building at 312 Azusa Street.[16] And on April 14, 1906, they had their first meeting in a building that had been a Methodist church and then had been sold and remodeled, the top half as apartments. When they acquired the building, the top floor was being used for storage and the bottom floor was used as a horse stable. They were offered the building for $8.00 a month.

A.G. Osterburg, a boss for a local construction company, paid several men to help renovate the building. Volunteers swept the floors and whitewashed the walls. J.V. McNeill, a devout Catholic and owner of the largest lumber company in Los Angeles, donated lumber for the cause. Sawdust was placed on the floor, and planks were nailed to wooden barrels for uses as pews. Two empty crates were nailed on top of each other to act as Seymour's pulpit.[17]

Four days after the opening of the Azusa Street mission, on April 18, the great earthquake of 1906 shook the foundations of San Francisco. Combined with the fire that erupted during the earthquake, the city of San Francisco was almost totally destroyed. Considering the apocalyptic size and destruction of the earthquake, along with the religious fervor in Los Angeles, the stage was set for a Holy Spirit eruption.

The previous year Frank Bartleman, a Holiness preacher from Pennsylvania, arrived in Los Angeles. After working with some of the churches, he found to his disappointment that many of the people were lukewarm and not ready for his long-desired revival. While in Los Angeles, Bartleman started to correspond with Evan Roberts about his passion for revival to come to California.

In June of 1905, Bartleman wrote that Los Angeles was truly a spiritual Jerusalem. He felt that this place would become the city where

God would pour out his Spirit. There was something there that inspired him, and he continued to give himself to prayer. He knew that the divisions among God's people were great hindrances to revival, and thus he wrote these words in his book, *Azusa Street*.

> Every fresh division or party in the church gives to the world a contradiction as to the oneness of the body of Christ, and the truthfulness of the Gospel. Multitudes are bowing down and burning incense to a doctrine rather than Christ. ...The Spirit is laboring for the unity of believers today, for the "one body," that the prayer of Jesus may be answered, "that they all may be one, that the world may believe."[18]

Bartleman attended the meetings on Bonnie Brae Street, and when they moved to 312 Azusa Street. He was there with them enjoying the warmth of Pentecostal fires. Bartleman, who was there at the beginning of the revival, best described those early days also in his book, *Azusa Street*:

> Brother Seymour generally sat behind two empty boxes, one on top of the other. He usually kept his head inside the top one during the meeting, in prayer. There was no pride there. The services ran almost continuously. Seeking souls could be found under the power almost any hour of the day or night. The place was never closed nor empty. The people came to meet God—He was always there. Hence a continuous meeting. The meeting did not depend on the human leader. God's presence became more and more wonderful. In that old building, with its low rafters and bare floors, God broke strong men and women to pieces, and put them together again for His glory. It was a tremendous overhauling process. Pride and self-assertion, self-importance, and self-esteem could not survive there. The religious ego preached its own funeral sermon quickly.

No subjects or sermons were announced ahead of time, and no special speakers for such an hour. No one knew what might be coming, what God would do. All was spontaneous, ordered by the Spirit. We wanted to hear from God, through whomever He might speak. We had no respect of persons. All were equal. No flesh might glory in His presence. He could not use the self-opinionated. Those were Holy Spirit meetings, led of the Lord. It had to start in poor surroundings to keep out the selfish, human element. All came down in humility together at His feet. They all looked alike and had all things in common, in that sense at least. The rafters were low, the tall must come down. By the time they got to Azusa, they were humbled, ready for the blessing. The fodder was thus placed for the lambs, not for giraffes. All could reach it.

We were delivered right there from ecclesiastical hierarchism and abuse. We wanted God. When we first reached the meeting, we avoided human contact and greeting as much as possible. We wanted to meet God first. We got our head under some bench in the corner in prayer, and met men only in the Spirit, knowing them "after the flesh" no more. The meetings started themselves, spontaneously, in testimony, praise, and worship. The testimonies were never hurried by a call for "popcorn." We had no prearranged program to be jammed through on time. Our time was the Lord's. We had real testimonies, from fresh heart-experience. Otherwise, the shorter the testimonies, the better. A dozen might be on their feet at one time, trembling under the mighty power of God. We did not have to get our cue from some leader; yet we were free from lawlessness. We were shut up to God in prayer in the meetings, our minds on Him.

All obeyed God, in meekness and humility. In honor we "preferred one another." The Lord was liable to burst through anyone. We prayed for this continually. Someone would finally get up, anointed for the message. All seemed to recognize this and gave way. It might be a child, a woman, or a man. It might be from the back seat or from the front. It made no difference. We rejoiced that God was working. No one wished to show himself. We thought only of obeying God. In fact, there was an atmosphere of God there that forbade anyone but a fool from attempting to put himself forward without the real anointing—and such did not last long. The meetings were controlled by the Spirit, from the throne. Those were truly wonderful days. I often said that I would rather live six months at that time than fifty years of ordinary life. But God is just the same today. Only we have changed.

Someone might be speaking. Suddenly the Spirit would fall upon the congregation. God Himself would give the altar call. Men would fall all over the house, like the slain in battle, or rush for the altar en masse to seek God. The scene often resembled a forest of fallen trees. Such a scene cannot be imitated. I never saw an altar call given in those early days. God Himself would call them. And the preacher knew when to quit. When He spoke, we all obeyed. It seemed a fearful thing to hinder or grieve the Spirit. The whole place was steeped in prayer. God was in His holy temple. It was for man to keep silent. The shekinah glory rested there. In fact, some claim to have seen the glory by night over the building. I do not doubt it. I have stopped more than once within two blocks of the place and prayed for strength before I dared go on. The presence of the Lord was so real.[19]

THE PURCHASE OF THE AZUSA MISSION

The work at Azusa was growing beyond expectations, and it became clear that the favor of the Lord was on that place. In the sixth volume of *The Apostolic Faith* newspaper, the announcement was published that they had purchased the property at 312 Azusa Street:

The Apostolic Faith Mission has purchased the lot and build-ings at 312 Azusa Street. Holy Spirit men have been elected as trustees, who hold the property.

The Apostolic Faith Mission at 312 Azusa Street
(Used by permission, Tim Enloe Library)

We believe the Lord chose this spot for His work, for He has wonderfully poured out His Spirit in the mission that started about a year ago from cottage prayer meetings where the Pentecost first fell. Now, through Spirit baptized ones who have gone out, and through papers published here, there has been raised up a mighty host. Praise God!

The property was purchased for $15,000, and $4,000 has already been paid down on it. Any friends wishing to have a share in buying this Mission for the Lord may send offerings to Brother Reuben Clark, who is secretary of the board of trustees.

It was necessary to buy this mission as a headquarters for the work, in order to hold it, as it would soon have been sold for other purposes. The situation is favorable, being centrally located and in surroundings where no one will be disturbed by prayers or shouts going up sometimes all night. Praise God!

The Mission building was formerly a place of worship where souls had been saved years ago, and the spot thus made sacred; and during the past year, hundreds have been saved, sanctified, healed, and baptized with the Holy Spirit. (Apostolic Faith Vol. 1, No. 6.)

THE COLOR LINE IS BROKEN

Whosoever will may come. Let brotherly love prevail. Azusa Street Mission
(Used by permission, Flower Pentecostal Heritage Center)

Initially, the Azusa Street mission had a multiracial, multiethnic character. The first issue of *The Apostolic Faith* newspaper reported that, "God makes no difference in nationality. Ethiopians, Chinese, Indians, Mexicans, and other nationalities worship together." One of the early Azusa Street leaders estimated that there were over 20 different nationalities in their meetings. "No instrument that God can use is rejected on account of color or dress or lack of education," was reported in the same issue of *The Apostolic Faith* paper. In the November issue Seymour wrote, "The meeting has been a melting time. The people are all melted together...made one lump, one bread, all one body in Christ Jesus.

THE AZUSA STREET REVIVAL

There is no Jew or Gentile, bond or free, in the Azusa Mission. No instrument that God can use is rejected on account of color or dress or lack of education. This is why God has built up the work…The sweetest thing is the loving harmony."

As Bartleman observed this melting of the races and the breaking down of racial prejudice, he would write that the blood of Jesus washed away the color line.

"There were far more white people than black people coming. The 'color line' was washed away in the blood." A.S. Worrell, translator of the New Testament, declared the Azusa work had rediscovered the blood of Christ to the Church at that time. Great emphasis was placed on Christ's blood, for cleansing, etc. A high standard was help up for a clean life. *"When the enemy shall come in like a flood, the spirit of the Lord shall lift up a standard against him"* (Isa. 59:19b KJV).[20]

WHEN HEAVEN INVADES EARTH

A few months after the revival had opened, hundreds were pouring into the little building on Azusa Street. Osterberg reported that as many as 21,300 attended the services, and up to 800 crowded into the building at a time. Every inch big enough for a chair was jammed full. *The Los Angeles Daily Times* reported, "The room was crowded almost to suffocation. Many were seated in the windows and scores who could not enter crowded around the lobby and struggled to view…."[21]

In one of the issues of *The Apostolic Faith* newspaper a man attending the Azusa Street meetings proclaimed, "I would have rather lived six months at that time than fifty years of ordinary life. I have stopped more than once within two blocks of the place and prayed for strength before I dared go on. The presence of the Lord was so real."[22]

*Leaders of the Azusa Street Mission: Seated (L-R) Sister Evans, Hiram Smith,
William Seymour, Clara Lum. Standing (L-R) Unidentified woman, Brother Evans, Jenny Moore,
(Seymour's future wife), Gleen Cook, Florence Crwaford, unidentified man, Sister Prince.
Florence Crawford's daughter is sitting on Hiram Smith's lap.
(Used by permission, Flower Pentecostal Heritage Center)*

Many of the newly baptized in the Holy Spirit would feel a call to the
mission field. Consequently, men and women were departing for
Scandinavia, China, India, Egypt, Ireland, and various other nations. Even
Sister Julia Hutchin, who initially locked Seymour out of her mission,
came to Azusa, received the baptism of the Holy Spirit, and left for Africa.[23]

At this time, everyone loved Seymour. When the Spirit moved, he
was known to keep his head inside the top box-crate in front of him,
bowed in prayer. He never asked for a salary, so he was continually
trusting God for his finances.

John G. Lake visited the Azusa Street meetings and in his book,
Adventures with God, wrote these words about Seymour:

"But I want to tell you, there were doctors, lawyers, and pro-
fessors listening to the marvelous things coming from his lips.
It was not what he said in words, it was what he said from his
spirit to my heart that showed me he had more of God in his

THE AZUSA STREET REVIVAL

life than any man I had ever met up to that time. It was God in Him that attracted the people.

One of the most remarkable features of the meetings was the "heavenly choir." A few, or as many as 20, would sing in their unknown tongue. There was no human orchestration. It was all under the direction of the Holy Spirit. Truly, heaven had come to earth."[24]

*In front of Azusa Street Mission: Back (L-R) Brother Sadams, F.F. Bosworth, Tom Hezmalhalah.
Front (L-R) William Seymour, John G. Lake
(Used by permission, Flower Pentecostal Heritage Center)*

ENDNOTES

1. http://www.believersweb.org/view.cfm?id=152

2. Liardon, *God's Generals*, 141.

3. Larry Martin, *The Life and Ministry of William Seymour* (Joplin, MO: Christian Life Books, 1999), 67-68.

4. http://www.ag.org/enrichmentjournal/199904/026_azusa_2.cfm

5. Liardon, *God's Generals*, 142.

6. Larry Martin, *The Life and Ministry of William Seymour*, 77.

7. Liardon, *God's Generals*, 142.

8. Martin, *The Life and Ministry of William Seymour*, 91.

9. Liardon, *God's Generals*, 143.

10. Martin, *The Life and Ministry of William Seymour*, 93.

11. Harvey Cox, *Fire from Heaven* (Cambridge: Da Copa Press, 1995), 50.

12. Anderson, *Vision of the Disinherited*, 61.

13. Ibid., 63.

14. Liardon, *God's Generals*, 144.

15. Liardon, *God's Generals*, 146.

16. Harvey Cox, *Fire from Heaven*, 56.

17. Liardon, *God's Generals*, 148.

18. Frank Bartleman, *Azusa Street* (Shippensburg, PA: Destiny Image, 2006).

19. Bartleman, *Azusa Street*, 6.

20. Bartleman, *Azusa Street*, 5.

21. Martin, *The Life and Ministry of William Seymour*, 117.

22. Bartleman, *Azusa Street*, 6.

23. Liardon, *God's Generals*, 151.

24. John G. Lake, *Adventures with God* (Tulsa, OK: Harrison House, 1981), 1819.

Chapter Five

WILLIAM SEYMOUR'S SERMONS

W ILLIAM Seymour was not the type who most people would
think of as an African-American Pentecostal preacher. He was
usually a meek man with a direct style that was not often dynamic in
presentation, but he could, however, become suddenly and volcanical-
ly emotional at times—in and out of the pulpit. Seymour saw himself
more as a teacher than a preacher.

The Azusa meetings were long, and on the whole they were spontaneous. In their early days music was a cappella, although one or two
instruments were included at times, and Jenny Evans would sometimes
play the piano during worship. There were songs; testimonies given by
visitors or read from those who had written them; prayer; and altar
calls for salvation, sanctification, or for baptism in the Holy Spirit. And
there was preaching. Sermons were generally not prepared in advance
but were typically spontaneous and inspired by the Spirit of God.

The meetings at the Apostolic Faith Mission quickly caught the
attention of the press due to the dynamic nature of the worship.
Between 300 and 350 people could get into the whitewashed, 40 by 60-
foot wood-frame structure, while many others were occasionally
forced to stand outside. Church services were held on the first floor
where the benches were placed in a rectangular pattern. Some of the
benches were simply planks put on top of empty nail kegs. There was
no elevated platform. There was no pulpit at the beginning of the
revival.

William Seymour studying the Scriptures
(Used by permission, Flower Pentecostal Heritage Center)

In the *Los Angeles Times*, Arthur Osterburg, the contractor who helped prepare the Mission for its meetings, described Brother Seymour:

> He was meek and plain spoken and no orator. He spoke the common language of the uneducated class. He might preach for three-quarters of an hour with no more emotionalism than that post. He was no arm-waving thunderer, by any stretch of the imagination. The only way to explain the results is this: that his teachings were so simple that people who were opposed to organized religion fell for it. It was the simplicity that attracted them.[1]

In September 1906, the first issue of *The Apostolic Faith* newspaper was printed and distributed at no cost—circulation quickly reached more than 50,000. Under the supervision of William Seymour, Florence Crawford (with the help of secretary Clara Lum and others) began keeping a record, in newspaper format, of what was said in the meetings. In the first issue of *The Apostolic Faith* are descriptions of the revival, testimonies of healing and deliverance, a personal note from Charles Parham, a listing of their doctrinal beliefs, a description of Seymour's call, and the recording of William Seymour's first sermon, "The Precious Atonement."

There are also teachings throughout the different issues that are not attributed to any particular author. In the 13 issues of *The Apostolic Faith*, there are 20 sermons directly noted as being written by Seymour. Eight of these sermons follow.

The Precious Atonement
(Vol. 1, No. 1)

Children of God, partakers of the precious atonement, let us study and see what there is in it for us.

First. Through the atonement we receive forgiveness of sins.

Second. We receive sanctification through the Blood of Jesus. "Wherefore Jesus also that he might sanctify the people with his own blood, suffered without the gate."

Sanctified from all original sin, we become sons of God. "For both he that sanctifies and they who are sanctified are all of one: for which cause he is not ashamed to call them brethren" (Heb. 2:11). (It seems that Jesus would be ashamed to call them brethren, if they were not sanctified.) Then you will not be ashamed to tell men and demons that you are sanctified, and are living a pure and holy life free from sin, a life that gives you power over the world, the flesh, and the devil. The devil does not like that kind of testimony. Through this precious atonement, we have freedom from all sin, though we are living in this world. We are permitted to sit in heavenly places in Christ Jesus.

Third. Healing of our bodies. Sickness and disease are destroyed through the precious atonement of Jesus. O how we ought to honor the stripes of Jesus, for "with his stripes we are healed." How we ought to honor that precious body which the Father sanctified and sent into the world, not simply set apart, but really sanctified, soul, body and spirit, free from sickness, disease and everything of the devil. A body that knew no sin and disease was given for these imperfect bodies of ours. Not only is the atonement for the sanctification of our souls, but also for the sanctification of our bodies from inherited disease. It matters not what has been in the blood. Every drop of blood we received from our mother is impure. Sickness is born in a child just as original sin is born in the child. He was manifested to destroy the works of the devil. Every sickness is of the devil.

Man in the Garden of Eden was pure and happy and knew no sickness till that unholy visitor came into the garden, then his whole system was poisoned and it has been flowing in the blood of all the human family down the ages till God spoke to His people and said, "I am the Lord that healeth thee." The children of Israel practiced divine healing. David, after being healed of rheumatism, (perhaps contracted in the caves where he hid himself from his pursuers,) testified saying, "Bless the Lord, O my soul, and all that is within me, bless His holy name, who forgives all thine iniquities, who healeth all thy diseases." David knew what it was to be healed. Healing continued with God's people till Solomon's heart was turned away by strange wives, and he brought in the black arts and mediums, and they went whoring after familiar spirits. God had been their healer, but after they lost the Spirit, they turned to the arm of flesh to find something to heal their diseases.

Thank God, we have a living Christ among us to heal our diseases. He will heal every case. The prophet had said, "With his stripes we are healed," and it was fulfilled when Jesus came. Also "He hath borne our griefs," (which means sickness, as translators tell us). Now if Jesus bore our sicknesses, why should we bear them? So, we get full salvation through the atonement of Jesus.

Fourth. And we get the baptism with the Holy Spirit and fire upon the sanctified life. We get Christ enthroned and crowned in our hearts. Let us lift up Christ to the world in all His fullness, not only in healing and salvation from all sin, but in His power to speak all the languages of the world. We need the triune God to enable us to do this.

We that are the messengers of this precious atonement ought to preach all of it, justification, sanctification, healing, the baptism with the Holy Spirit, and signs following. "How shall we escape if we neglect so great salvation?" God is now confirming His Word by granting signs and wonders to follow the preaching of the Full Gospel in Los Angeles.

—W.J. Seymour

COUNTERFEITS
(VOL. 1, NO. 4)

God has told us in His precious word that we should know a tree by its fruit.

Wherever we find the real, we find the counterfeit also. But praise God for the real.

We find in the time of Peter, when men and women were receiving the power of the Holy Ghost, the counterfeit appeared in Annanias and Saphira. But God's power was mightier than all the forces of hell, so their sin found them out. Be careful, dear loved ones for your sin will surely find you out. "But if we walk in the light as He is in the light, we have fellowship one with another and the blood of Jesus Christ his Son cleanseth us from all sin."

In our meetings, we have had people to come and claim that they had received the baptism with the Holy Spirit, but when they were put to the test by the Holy Spirit, they were found wanting. So they got down and got saved and sanctified and baptized with the Holy Spirit and spoke in tongues by the Holy Spirit. And again people have imitated the gift of tongues, but how quickly the Holy Spirit would reveal to every one of the true children that had the Pentecostal baptism, and put a heavy rebuke upon the counterfeit, in tongues, until the counterfeits were silenced and condemned. God's promises are true and sure.

People are trying to imitate the work of the Holy Ghost these days, just as they did when the Lord sent Moses to Pharaoh in Ex. 7,8, and gave him a miracle or sign to show before Pharaoh, that when Aaron should cast his rod before Pharaoh, it should become a serpent. So when Pharaoh saw that Aaron's rod had become a serpent, he called for his wise men and the counterfeit sorcerers and magicians of Egypt. They also did in like manner with their enchantments, for they cast down every man his rod, and they became serpents, but Aaron's rod swallowed up their rods. So the power of the Holy Ghost in God's people today condemns and swallows up the counterfeit. It digs up and exposes all the power of Satan—Christian Science, Theosophy, and Spiritualism—all are uncovered before the Son of God. Glory to God.

Spiritualists have come to our meetings and had the demons cast out of them and have been saved and sanctified. Christian Scientists have come to the meetings and had the Christian Science demons cast out of them and have accepted the blood. Every plant that my heavenly Father hath not planted shall be rooted up. People have come to this place full of demons and God has cast them out, and they have gone out crying with loud voices. Then when all the demons were cast out, they got saved, sanctified, and baptized with the Holy Ghost, clothed in their right minds and filled with glory and power. Dear loved ones, it is not by might nor by power but by my Spirit, saith the Lord. "Tarry ye in the city of Jerusalem, until ye be endued with power from on high. John truly baptized with water, but ye shall be baptized with the Holy Ghost not many days hence." These were Jesus departing words. May you tarry until you receive your personal Pentecost. Amen.

—W. J. Seymour

Receive Ye the Holy Spirit
(Vol. 1, No. 5)

1. The first step in seeking the Baptism of the Holy Spirit, is to have a clear knowledge of the new birth in our souls that is the first work of grace and brings everlasting life to our souls. "Therefore being justified by faith, we have peace with God." Every one of us that repents of our sins and turns to the Lord Jesus with faith in Him, receives forgiveness of sins. Justification and regeneration are simultaneous. The pardoned sinner becomes a child of God in justification.

2. The next step for us is to have a clear knowledge, by the Holy Spirit, of the second work of grace wrought in our hearts by the power of the Blood and the Holy Spirit. Hebrews 10:14-15, "For by one offering, He hath perfected forever them that are sanctified, whereof the Holy Spirit also is a witness to us." The Scripture also teaches (Hebrews 2:11), "For both He that sanctifies and they who are sanctified are all of one; for which cause He is not ashamed to call them brethren." We have Christ crowned and enthroned in our hearts, the tree of life. We have the brooks and streams of salvation flowing in our souls, but praise God, we can have the rivers. For the Lord Jesus says, "He that believeth on me, as the Scripture hath said, out of his innermost being shall flow rivers of living water. This spoke He of the Spirit, for the Holy Spirit was not yet given." However, praise our God, He is now given and being poured out upon all flesh. All races, nations, and tongues are receiving the Baptism of the Holy Spirit and fire, according to the prophecy of Joel.

3. When we have a clear knowledge of justification and sanctification, through the precious Blood of Jesus Christ in our hearts, then we can be a recipient of the Baptism of the Holy Spirit. Many people today are sanctified, cleansed from all sin, and perfectly consecrated to God, but they have never obeyed the Lord according to Acts 1:4,5,8 and Luke 24:39, for their real personal Pentecost, the enduement of power for service and work and for sealing unto the day of redemption. The

Baptism of the Holy Spirit is a gift without repentance, upon the sanctified, cleansed vessel. 2 Corinthians 1:21-22, "Now He which established us with you in Christ, and hath anointed us, is God, who hath also sealed us, and given the earnest of the Spirit in our hearts." Praise our God for the sealing of the Holy Spirit unto the day of redemption.

Dearly beloved, the only people that will meet our Lord and Savior Jesus Christ and go with Him into the marriage supper of the Lamb, are the wise virgins—not only saved and sanctified, with pure and clean hearts, but having the Baptism of the Holy Spirit. The others we find will not be prepared. They have some oil in their lamps but they have not the double portion of His Holy Spirit.

The disciples were filled with the unction of the Holy Spirit before Pentecost, which sustained them until they received the Holy Spirit baptism. Many people today are filled with joy and gladness, but they are far from the enduement of power. Sanctification brings rest, sweetness, and quietness to our souls. We are one with the Lord Jesus and are able to obey His precious Word, that "Man shall not live by bread alone, but by every word that proceedeth out of the mouth of God," and we are feeding upon Christ.

However, let us wait for the promise of the Father upon our souls. According to Jesus' Word, "John truly baptized with water, but ye shall be baptized with the Holy Spirit not many days hence Ye shall receive power after that the Holy Spirit is come upon you; and ye shall be witnesses unto me, both in Jerusalem and in all Judea, and in Samaria, and unto the uttermost part of the earth" (Acts 1:5-8). Glory! Glory! Hallelujah! Oh, worship, get down on your knees and ask the Holy Spirit to come in, and you will find Him right at your heart's door, and He will come in. Prove Him now. Amen.

—W. J. Seymour

GIFTS OF THE SPIRIT
(VOL. 1, NO. 5)

"Now concerning spiritual gifts brethren, I would not have you ignorant."

Paul was speaking to the Corinthian Church at this time. They were like Christ's people everywhere today. Many of His people do not know their privileges in this blessed Gospel. The Gospel of Christ is the power of God unto salvation to everyone that believeth. And in order that we might know His power, we must forever abide in the Word of God that we may have the precious fruits of the Spirit, and not only the fruits but the precious gifts that Father has for His little ones.

Dearly beloved, may we search the Scriptures and see for ourselves whether we are measuring up to every word that proceedeth out of the mouth of God. If we will remain in the Scriptures and follow the blessed Holy Spirit all the way, we will be able to measure up to the Word of God in all of its fullness. Paul prayed in Eph. 3:16[-20], "That He would grant you, according to the riches of His glory, to be strengthened with might by His Spirit in the inner man; that Christ may dwell in your hearts by faith; that ye being rooted and grounded in love, may be able to comprehend with all saints, what is the breadth, and length, and depth, and height, and to know the love of Christ which passeth knowledge; that ye might be filled with all the fullness of God. Now unto Him that is able to do exceeding abundantly above all that we ask or think, according to the power that worketh in us."

Many people say today that tongues are the least gift of any that the Lord can give, and they do not need it, and ask, "What good is it to us?" By careful study of the Word, we see in the 14th [chapter] of [First] Corinthians, Paul telling the church to "follow after charity and desire spiritual gifts." Charity means Divine love without which we will never be able to enter heaven. Gifts all will fall, but Divine love will last through all eternity. And right in the same verse he says, "Desire spiritual gifts, but rather that ye may prophesy," that is to say, preach in your own tongue that will build up the saints and the church.

But he says in the next verse, "For he that speaketh in an unknown tongue, speaketh not unto men, but unto God, for no man understandeth him, howbeit in the Spirit, he speaketh mysteries," (R. V.—hidden truth.) "But he that prophesieth speaketh unto man to edification, exhortation and comfort." He that prophesies in his own tongue edifies the church; but he that speaks in unknown tongues edifies himself. His spirit is being edified, while the church is not edified, because they do not understand what he says unless the Lord gives somebody the interpretation of the tongue.

Here is where many stumble that have not this blessed gift to use in the Spirit. They say, What good is it when you do not know what you are talking about? Praise God, every gift He gives is a good gift. It is very blessed, for when the Lord gets ready, He can speak in any language He chooses to speak. You ask, "Is not prophecy the best gift?" Prophecy is the best gift to the church, for it builds up the saints and edifies them and exalts them to higher things in the Lord Jesus. If a brother or sister is speaking in tongues and cannot speak any English, but preaches altogether in tongues, and has no interpretation, they are less than he that prophesies [sic]. But, if they interpret they are just as great.

May God help all of His precious people to read the 14th [chapter] of I Cor., and give them the real interpretation of the Word. May we all use our gift to the glory of God and not worship the gift. The Lord gives us power to use it to His own glory and honor. Many times, when we were receiving this blessed Pentecost, we all used to break out in tongues; but we have learned to be quieter with the gift. Often when God sends a blessed wave upon us, we all may speak in tongues for awhile, but we will not keep it up while preaching service is going on, for we want to be obedient to the Word, that everything may be done decently and in order and without confusion. Amen.

—W. J. Seymour

THE BAPTISM WITH THE HOLY GHOST
(VOL. 1, NO. 6)

Dear ones in Christ who are seeking the baptism with the Holy Ghost: do not seek for tongues but for the promise of the Father, and pray for the baptism with the Holy Ghost, and God will throw in the tongues according to Acts 2. 4. We read in Acts 1. 4, 5, "And being assembled together with them, commanded them that they should not depart from Jerusalem, but wait for the promise of the Father, which, saith He, ye have heard of me. For John truly baptized with water; but ye shall be baptized with the Holy Ghost not many days hence."

This promise of the Father was preached unto the disciples by John the Baptist. And Jesus reminded the disciples about this baptism that John had preached to them in life. In England we find the same thing. Math. 3, 11 [Matthew 3:11]. John, after warning the Jews and Pharisees against sin and hypocrisy, preached the doctrine of the baptism with the Holy Ghost. He said first, "Bring forth therefore, fruits meet for repentance." God is sending our [sic] His precious ministers to preach repentance to the people and turn them from their sins and cause them to make restitution according to their ability, and to have faith in the Lord Jesus Christ and be saved. Glory to God!

And then they must get sanctified through the precious Blood of Jesus Christ, for He says in John 17. 14-19, "I pray not that Thou shouldst keep them from the evil. They are not of the world, even as I am not of the world. Sanctify them through Thy truth; Thy Word is truth. As Thou hast sent Me into the world, even so have I also sent them into the world. And for their sakes I sanctify Myself, that they also might be sanctified through the truth." God wants His people to be sanctified, because He says again in Heb. 13. 12, "Wherefore Jesus also that He might sanctify the people with His own Blood, suffered without the gate. Let us go forth therefore unto Him without the camp, bearing His reproach."

Then Jesus taught the disciples to tarry at Jerusalem. They obeyed Him and waited for the promise of the Father. "And when the day of Pentecost was fully come, they were all with one accord in one place. And suddenly there came a sound from heaven as of a rushing, mighty wind, and it filled all the house where they were sitting. And there appeared unto them cloven tongues like as of fire, and it sat upon each of them.

And they were all filled with the Holy Ghost, and began to speak with other tongues, as the Spirit gave them utterance." Acts 2, 1-4. Wind is always typical of the Spirit or of life. "And it filled all the house where they were sitting." The rivers of salvation had come and had filled the whole place, and they all were immersed or baptized in the Holy Spirit. Praise God! "And there appeared unto them cloven tongues like as of fire." Beloved, when we receive the baptism with the Holy Ghost and fire, we surely will speak in tongues as the Spirit gives utterance. We are not seeking for tongues, but we are seeking the baptism with the Holy Ghost and fire. And when we receive it, we shall be so filled with the Holy Ghost, that He Himself will speak in the power of the Spirit.

"And they were all filled with the Holy Ghost, and began to speak with other tongues, as the Spirit gave them utterance." Now, beloved, do not be too concerned about your speaking in tongues, but let the Holy Ghost give you utterance, and it will come just as freely as the air we breathe. It is nothing worked up, but it comes from the heart. "With the heart man believeth unto righteousness; and with the mouth, confession is made unto salvation." So when the Holy Ghost life comes in, the mouth opens, through the power of the Spirit in the heart. Glory to God!

"There were, dwelling at Jerusalem, Jews, devout men, out of every nation under heaven. Now when this was noised abroad, the multitude came together, and were confounded, because that every man heard them speak in his own language. And they were all amazed and marveled, saying one to another, Behold, are not all these which speak,

Gallileans. And how hear we every man speak in our own tongue wherein we were born?" Acts. 2. 5-8.

Beloved, if you do not know the language that you speak, do not puzzle yourself about it, for the Lord did not promise us He would tell us what language we were speaking, but He promised us the interpretation of what we speak. In seeking the baptism, first get a clear, definite witness in your soul that you have the abiding Christ within. Then there will be no trouble in receiving the Pentecostal baptism, through faith in our Lord and Savior, Jesus Christ, for it is a free gift that comes without repentance. Bless His holy name!

—W. J. Seymour

LETTER TO ONE SEEKING THE HOLY GHOST
(VOL. 1, NO. 9)

Dear Beloved in Christ Jesus:

The Lord Jesus has said in His precious Word, "Blessed are they which do hunger and thirst after righteousness, for they shall be filled." Matt. 5, 6. God's promises are true and sure. We can rest upon His promises. He says, "Blessed are the pure in heart, for they shall see God." Matt. 5, 8. "Blessed are the poor in spirit, for theirs is the kingdom of heaven." Matt. 5, 3.

The Lord Jesus is always ready to fill the hungry, thirsty soul, for He said in His precious Word, "He that believeth on Me as the scripture hath said, out of his innermost being shall flow rivers of living water. (But this spoke He of the Spirit which they that believe on Him should receive: for the Holy Ghost was not yet given; because that Jesus was not yet glorified.)" John 7. 38, 39. But, praise God, He is given to us today.

All we have to do is to obey the first chapter of Acts, and wait for the promise of the Father upon our souls. The Lord Jesus said in His precious Word, "Behold I send the promise of My Father upon you; but tarry ye in the city of Jerusalem until ye be endued with power from on high. (Luke 24, 49.) For John truly baptized with water; but ye shall be baptized with the Holy Ghost not many days hence."

"Ye shall receive power after that the Holy Ghost is come upon you; and ye shall be witnesses unto Me both in Jerusalem and in all Judea, and in Samaria and unto the uttermost part of the earth." Acts I. 5, 8. They tarried until they received the mighty power of the baptism with the Holy Spirit upon their souls. Then God put the credentials in their hearts, and put the ring of authority on their finger, and sealed them in the forehead with the Father's name, and wrote on their heart the name of the New Jerusalem, and put in their hand the stone with the name written that no man knoweth save he that receiveth it. Praise the Lord, for His mercy endureth forever. Let us stand upon His promises. They are sure, they will not break.

The Lord Jesus says, "Behold, I give you power to tread on serpents and scorpions and over all the power of the enemy; and nothing shall by any means hurt you." Luke 10, 19. Dear loved one, the Lord Jesus when He rose from the dead, said "All power is given unto Me in heaven and in earth. Go ye therefore, and teach all nations, baptizing them in the name of the Father, and of the Son, and of the Holy Ghost. (Matt. 28. 19) He that believeth and is baptized shall be saved; but he that believeth not shall be damned. And these signs shall follow them that believe; in My name shall they cast out devils; they shall speak with new tongues; they shall take up serpents; and if they drink any deadly thing, it shall not hurt them; they shall lay hands on the sick and they shall recover." Mark 16: 16-18. And they went forth and preached everywhere, the Lord working with them, and confirming the Word with signs following. Praise His dear name, for He is just the same today.

The first thing in order to receive this precious and wonderful baptism with the Holy Spirit, we want to have a clear knowledge of justification by faith according to the Bible. Rom. 5:1, "Therefore being justified by faith, we have peace with God through our Lord Jesus

Christ," faith that all our actual sins may be washed away. Actual sin means committed sin.

And then the second step is to have a real knowledge of sanctification, which frees us from original sin—the sin that we were born with, which we inherited from our father Adam. We were not responsible for that sin until we received light, for we could not repent of a sin that we did not commit. When we came to the Lord as a sinner, we repented to God of our actual sins, and God for Christ's sake pardoned us and washed our sin and pollution away, and planted eternal life in our souls.

Afterwards we saw in the Word of God, "This is the will of God, even your sanctification." I Thess. 4:3, also John 17:15-19. We consecrated ourselves to God, and the Lord Jesus sanctified our souls, and made us every whit clean.

Then after we were clearly sanctified, we prayed to God for the baptism with the Holy Spirit. So He sent the Holy Spirit to our hearts and filled us with His blessed Spirit, and He gave us the Bible evidence, according to the 2nd chapter of Acts verses 1 to 4, speaking with other tongues as the Spirit gives utterance.

Praise our God, He is the same yesterday, today, and forever. Receive Him just now and He will fill you. Amen. Don't get discouraged but pray until you are filled, for the Lord says, "Men ought always to pray and not to faint." Don't stop because you do not receive the baptism with the Holy Ghost at the first, but continue until you are filled. The Lord Jesus told His disciples to tarry until they were endued with power from on high. Many people today are willing to tarry just so long, and then they give up and fail to receive their personal Pentecost that would measure with the Bible. The Lord Jesus says, "Ye shall be filled." He says that to the person that hungers and thirsts after righteousness and He says they are blessed. So if there is a hunger and thirst in our souls for righteousness, we are blest of Him. Praise His dear name!

Yours in Christ,
—W. J. Seymour

THE BAPTISM WITH THE HOLY GHOST
(VOL. 1, NO. 12)

The Azusa standard of the baptism with the Holy Ghost is according to the Bible in Acts 1:5,8; Acts 2:4 and Luke 24:49. Bless His holy name. Hallelujah to the Lamb for the baptism with the Holy Ghost and fire and speaking in tongues as the Spirit gives utterance. Jesus gave the church at Pentecost a great lesson of how to carry on a revival, and it would be well for every church to follow Jesus' standard of the baptism with the Holy Ghost and fire.

"And when the day of Pentecost was fully come, they were all with one accord in one place." O, beloved, there is where the secret is: one accord, one place, one heart, one soul, one mind, one prayer. If God can get a people anywhere in one accord and in one place, of one heart, mind, and soul, believing for this great power, it will fall and Pentecostal results will follow. Glory to God!

Apostolic Faith doctrine means one accord, one soul, one heart. May God help every child of His to live In Jesus' prayer: "That they all may be one, as Thou, Father, art in Me and I In Thee; that they all may be one to us; that the world may believe that Thou hast sent Me." Praise God! O, how my heart cries out to God in these days that He would make every child of His see the necessity of living in the 17th chapter of John, that we may be one in the body of Christ, as Jesus has prayed.

When we are sanctified through the truth, then we are one in Christ, and we can get into one accord for the gift or power of the Holy Ghost, and God will come in like a rushing mighty wind and fill every heart with the power of the Holy Spirit. Glory to His holy name. Bless God! O, how I praise Him for this wonderful salvation that is spreading over this great earth. The baptism of the Holy Ghost brings the glory of God to our hearts.

The Holy Ghost Is Power

There is a great difference between a sanctified person and one that is baptized with the Holy Ghost and fire. A sanctified person is cleansed and filled with divine love, but the one that is baptized with the Holy Ghost has the power of God on his soul and has power with God and men, power over all the kingdoms of Satan and over all his emissaries. God can take a worm and thresh a mountain. Glory to God. Hallelujah!

In all Jesus' great revivals and mircles [sic], the work was wrought by the power of the Holy Ghost flowing through His sanctified humanity. When the Holy Ghost comes and takes us as His instruments, this is the power that convicts men and women and causes them to see that there is a reality in serving Jesus Christ. O, beloved, we ought to thank God that He has made us the tabernacles of the Holy Ghost. When you have the Holy Ghost, you have an empire, a power within yourself. Elijah was a power in himself through the Holy Ghost. He brought down fire from heaven. So when we get the power of the Holy Ghost, we will see the heavens open and the Holy Ghost power falling on earth, power over sickness, diseases and death.

The Lord never revoked the commission He gave to His disciples: "Heal the sick, cleanse the lepers, raise the dead," and He is going to perform these things if He can get a people in unity. The Holy Spirit is power with God and man. You have power with God as Elijah had. God put man over all His works; but we know that when Adam sinned, he lost a great deal of his power; but now through the Blood of Jesus, He says, "Behold, I give you power to tread on serpents and scorpions, and over all the powers of the enemy." The Lord Jesus wants a church, when He comes back to earth, just like the one He started when He left the earth and organized it on the day of Pentecost.

Tarry in One Accord

O, may every child of God seek his real personal Pentecost, stop quibbling and come to the standard that Jesus laid down for us in Acts 2:

"And suddenly there came a sound from heaven as of a rushing mighty wind, and it filled all the house where they were sitting." Glory to God! O, beloved, if you wait on God for this baptism of the Holy Ghost just now, and can get two or three people together that are sanctified through the Blood of Christ, and all get into one accord, God will send the baptism of the Holy Ghost upon your souls as the rain falls from heaven. You may not have a preacher to come to you and preach the doctrine of the Holy Ghost and fire, but you can obey Jesus' saying in the passage. "Where two or three are gathered together in My name, there am I in the midst of them." This is Jesus' baptism; and if two or three are gathered together in His name and pray for the baptism of the Holy Ghost, they can have it this day or this night because it is the promise of the Father. Glory to God!

This was the Spirit that filled the house as a rushing mighty wind. The Holy Ghost is typified by wind, air, breath, life, fire. "And there appeared unto them cloven tongues like as of fire, and it sat upon each of them; and they were all filled with the Holy Ghost and began to speak with other tongues as the Spirit gave them utterance." So, beloved, when you get your personal Pentecost, the signs will follow in speaking with tongues as the Spirit gives utterance. This is true. Wait on God and you will find it a truth in your own life. God's promises are true and sure.

The Baptism Falls on a Clean Heart

Jesus is our example. "And Jesus being full of the Holy Ghost, returned from

Jordan, and was led by the Spirit." We find in reading the Bible that the baptism with the Holy Ghost and fire falls on a clean, sanctified life, for we see according to the Scriptures that Jesus was "holy, harmless, undefiled," and filled with wisdom and favor with God and man, before God anointed Him with the Holy Ghost and power. For in Luke 2:40 we read, "Jesus waxed strong in spirit, filled with wisdom, and the grace of

God was upon Him"; and in Luke 2:52, "And Jesus increased in wisdom and stature, and in favor with God and man."

After Jesus was empowered with the Holy Ghost at Jordan, He returned in the power of the Spirit into Galilee, and there went out a fame of Him through all the region round about. Glory to God! He was not any more holy or any more meak [sic], but had greater authority. "And He taught in their synagogues, being glorified of all."

Beloved, If Jesus who was God Himself, heeded the Holy Ghost to empower Him for His ministry and His miracles, how much more do we children need the Holy Ghost baptism today. O, that men and women would tarry for the baptism with the Holy Ghost and fire upon their souls, that the glory may be seen upon them just as it was upon the disciples on the day of Pentecost in the fiery emblem of tongues.

The tongues of fire represented the great Shekina glory. So today the Shekina glory rests day and night upon those who are baptized with the Holy Ghost, while He abides in their souls. For His presence is with us. Glory to His name. I thank Him for this wonderful salvation. Let us ring His praises through all the world that all men may know that the Comforter has come. Bless His dear name!

Jesus' First Sermon After His Baptism

"And He came to Nazareth where He was brought up: and as His custom was, He went into the synagogue on the Sabbath day and stood up for to read. And there was delivered unto Him the book of the prophet Esaias. And when He had opened the book, He found the place where it is written, 'The Spirit of the Lord is upon Me because He hath anointed Me to preach the Gospel to the poor: He hath sent me to heal the brokenhearted, to preach deliverance to the captives, and recovering of sight to the blind, to set at liberty them that are bruised, to preach the acceptable year of the Lord'" (Luke 4:18-19). Hallelujah. Glory to God! This is Jesus' sermon after His baptism with the Holy Ghost, preaching in the synagogue. He acknowledged that the Spirit of God was upon Him.

Jesus was the Son of God and born of the Holy Ghost and filled with the Holy

Ghost from His mother's womb: but the baptism with the Holy Ghost came upon His sanctified humanity at the Jordan. In His humanity, He needed the Third Person of the Trinity to do His work. And He could truly say that His fingers became instruments of the Holy Ghost to cast out devils.

The Holy Spirit Flows Through Pure Channels

If men and women today will consecrate themselves to God, and get their hands and feet and eyes and affections, body and soul, all sanctified, how the Holy Ghost will use such people. He will find pure channels to flow through sanctified avenues for His power. People will be saved, sanctified, healed and baptized with the Holy Ghost and fire.

The baptism with the Holy Ghost comes through our Lord and Savior Jesus Christ by faith in His word. In order to receive it, we must first be sanctified. Then we can become His witnesses unto the uttermost parts of the earth. You will never have an experience to measure with Acts 2:4 and 16, 17, until you get your personal Pentecost or the baptism with the Holy Ghost and fire (Matthew 3:11).

This is the latter rain that God is pouring out upon His humble children in the last days. We are preaching a Gospel that measures with the great commission that Jesus gave His disciples on the day when He arose from the dead (Matthew 28:19-20). "Go ye therefore and teach all nations, baptizing them in the name of the Father, and of the Son, and of the Holy Ghost: teaching them to observe all things whatsoever I have commanded you: and lo, I am with you always, even unto the end of the world. Amen!" They received the power to measure with this commission on the day of Pentecost (Acts 2:4). Bless the lord. O, how I bless God to see His mighty power manifested in these last days. God wants His people to receive the baptism with the Holy Ghost and fire.

—W. J. Seymour

THE HOLY GHOST AND THE BRIDE
(VOL. II, NO. 13)

We read in Rev. 22:17, "The Spirit and the Bride say, 'Come'." O, how sweet it is for us to have this blessed privilege of being a coworker with the Holy Ghost. He inspires us with faith in God's word and endues us with power for service for the Master. Bless His dear name!

Every man and woman that receives the baptism with the Holy Ghost is the bride of Christ. They have a missionary spirit for saving souls. They have the spirit of

Pentecost. Glory to God!

"And let him that heareth say, come: and let him that is athirst, come; and whosoever will, let him take the water of life freely." O, what a blessed text. The bride of Christ is calling the thirsty to come to Jesus because this is the work of the Holy Ghost in the believer. He intercedes for the lost: He groans for them.

The Spirit also calls the believer to come to Jesus and get sanctified. He points the sanctified to Jesus for his baptism with the Holy Ghost. When you are baptized with the Holy Ghost, you will have power to call sinners to Jesus, and they will be saved, and sanctified, and baptized with the Holy Ghost and fire. Amen!

Christ's bride is pure and spotless, "Thou art all fair, my love, there is no spot in thee" (Sol. Songs, 4:7). Christ's bride is clean, free from sin and all impurity. He gave Himself for her, that He might sanctify and cleanse the church with the washing of water by the Word. That He might present it to Himself a glorious church, not having spot or wrinkle or any such thing, but that it should be holy and without blemish (Eph. 5:25, 27).

Christ's bride has but one husband (2 Cor., 11:2). She is subject to Him (Eph., 5:25).

The Bridegroom is the Son of God (2 Cor., 11:2).

We are married to Christ now in the Spirit, (Rom., 7:2-4). Not only when He comes are we married to Christ, but also right now, if you are sanctified and baptized with the Holy Ghost and fire, you are married to Him already. God has a people to measure up to the Bible standard in this great salvation. Bless His holy name. Amen!

—W. J. Seymour

ENDNOTE

1. Robert Owens, *Speak to the Rock* (Lanham, MD: University Press of America, 1998), 57.

Chapter Six

AZUSA STREET TESTIMONIES

FORTUNATELY, *The Apostolic Faith* newspapers were preserved for us, and we can now look back a hundred years trying to understand all that took place in that little mission at 312 Azusa Street. You have read about the many events leading up to April 1906 and about the fire that fell in Los Angeles on those gathered together in the Azusa meetings. Now you will experience a little taste of how thousands of lives were changed at the Azusa meetings—salvations, deliverances, people baptized in the Spirit, missionaries sent to other parts of the world, and the spread of the Azusa fire to almost every corner of the earth. The following accounts were recorded in *The Apostolic Faith* newspaper.

THE APOSTOLIC FAITH
VOL. 1, NO. 1

Canes, crutches, medicine bottles, and glasses are being thrown aside as God heals. That is the safe way. No need to keep an old crutch or medicine bottle of any kind around after God heals you. Some, in keeping some such appliance as a souvenir, have been tempted to use them again and have lost their healing.

We cannot tell how many people have been saved, and sanctified, and baptized with the Holy Spirit, and healed of all manner of sicknesses. Many are speaking in new tongues, and some are on their way to the foreign fields with the gift of the language. We are going on to get more of the power of God.

Many have laid aside their glasses and had their eyesight perfectly restored. The deaf have had their hearing restored.

A man was healed of asthma of twenty years standing. Many have been healed of heart trouble and lung trouble.

Many are saying that God has given the message that He is going to shake Los Angeles with an earthquake. First, there will be a revival to give all an opportunity to be saved. The revival is now in progress.

The Lord has given the gift of writing in unknown languages, also the gift of playing on instruments.

A little girl who walked with crutches and had tuberculosis of the bones, as the doctors declared, was healed and dropped her crutches and began to skip about the yard.

All over this city, God has been setting homes on fire and coming down and melting, saving, sanctifying and baptizing with the Holy Spirit.

Many churches have been praying for Pentecost, and Pentecost has come. The question is, will they accept it? God has answered in a way they did not look for. He came in a humble way as of old, born in a manger.

The secular papers have been stirred and published reports against the movement, but it has only resulted in drawing hungry souls who understand that the devil would not fight a thing unless God was in it. They have come and found it was indeed the power of God.

Jesus was too large for the synagogue. He preached outside because there was not room for Him inside. This Pentecostal movement is too large to be confined in any denomination or sect. It works outside, drawing all together in one bond of love, one church, and one body of Christ.

A Mohammedan [sic. Muslim], a Sudanese by birth, a man who is an interpreter and speaks sixteen languages, came into the meetings at Azusa Street and the Lord gave him messages which none but himself could understand. He identified, interpreted and wrote several languages.

A brother who had been a spiritualist medium and who was so possessed with demons that he had no rest, and was on the point of committing suicide, was instantly delivered of demon power. He then sought God for the pardon of his sins and sanctification, and is now filled with a different spirit.

A little girl about twelve years of age was sanctified in a Sunday afternoon children's meeting, and in the evening meeting she was baptized with the Holy Spirit. When she was filled those standing near remarked, "Who can doubt such a clear case of God's power?"

Nearly an hour and a half later, a young man was converted, sanctified, and baptized with the Holy Spirit, and spoke with tongues. He was also healed from consumption, so that when he visited the doctor he pronounced his lungs sound. He has received many tongues, also the gift of prophecy, and writing in a number of foreign languages, and has a call to a foreign field.

Many are the prophecies spoken in unknown tongues and many the visions that God is giving concerning His soon coming. The heathen must first receive the Gospel. One prophecy given in an unknown tongue was interpreted, "The time is short, and I am going to send out a large number in the Spirit of God to preach the Full Gospel in the power of the Spirit."

About 160 people in Los Angeles, more than on the day of Pentecost, have received the gift of the Holy Spirit and the Bible evidence, the gift of tongues, and many have been saved and sanctified, nobody knows how many. People are seeking at the altar three times a day and it is hard to close at night because of seekers and those who are under the power of God.

When Pentecostal lines are struck, Pentecostal giving commences. Hundreds of dollars have been laid down for the sending of missionaries and thousands will be laid down. No collections are taken for rent, no begging for money. No man's silver or gold is coveted. The silver and the gold are His own to carry on His work. He can also publish his own papers without asking for money or subscription price.

In the meetings, it is noticeable that while some in the rear are opposing and arguing, others are at the altar falling down under the power of God and feasting on the good things of God. The two spirits are always manifest, but no opposition can kill, and no power in earth or hell can stop God's work, while He has consecrated instruments through which to work.

Many have received the gift of singing as well as speaking in the inspiration of the Spirit. The Lord is giving new voices, He translates old songs into new tongues, He gives the music that is being sung by the angels and He has a heavenly choir all singing the same heavenly song in harmony. It is beautiful music; no instruments are needed in the meetings.

The gift of languages is given with the commission, "Go ye into all the world and preach the Gospel to every creature." The Lord has given languages to the unlearned Greek, Latin, Hebrew, French, German, Italian, Chinese, Japanese, Zulu and languages of Africa, Hindu and Bengali and dialects of India, Chippewa and other languages of the Indians, Eskimo, and the deaf mute language. In fact, the Holy Spirit speaks all the languages of the world through His children.

In the City of Oakland, during the five weeks that the band from Los Angeles was there, Brother and Sister Evans and Sister Florence Crawford, sixty-five souls received the baptism with the Holy Spirit, and thirty were sanctified and nineteen converted.

THE APOSTOLIC FAITH
VOL. 1, NO. 3

The Lord is saving drunkards and taking the appetite for liquor and tobacco completely away.

Reports come from Denver that forty souls have received the Pentecost and are speaking in tongues.

A young man saved from the morphine habit has no more desire for the stuff and gave up his instruments.

Four workers from Texas, Brother and Sister Oyler and Brother and Sister Quinton have arrived in Los Angeles lately. God has been using them in Whittier.

Brother Tom Qualis from Fresno said, "I came 300 miles to this meeting and I feel heaven in my soul. It seems to me I am getting some of the crumbs that fall from Father's table. I feel the presence of God here."

"Cartoons in the newspapers were my first introduction to this meeting," said a brother, "and I said, this is what I have been praying for years. I was warned by leaders that it was of the devil, but I came and got a touch of heaven in my soul."

A brother had a vision of fires springing up and then gathering together and advancing in a solid wall of flame. A preacher was trying to put it out with a wet gunny sack, but it was evident there was no use fighting it. Our God is marching on. Hallelujah. The man with the wet gunny sack is here also, but his efforts only call attention to the fire.

The blind man who was saved and had his sight restored was saved because of hearing a few praying in tongues in a cottage meeting. He was a sinner; a very profane man, and was convicted because of tongues. Praise God for His marvelous works to the children of men.

THE APOSTOLIC FAITH
VOL. 1, NO. 5

THREW AWAY HIS CRUTCHES
Report of a Case of Healing in Oakland
The Man was a Sinner on whom This Miracle Was Shown
Oakland, Cal, Dec. 18th.

A wonderful miracle of healing took place at the tent yesterday afternoon. Bro. Manley's lesson was on divine healing and he emphasized the statement that God healed sinners. As if to corroborate his testimony, when he had closed, a rough looking man arose with a crutch under one arm and a cane in the other hand. He said in substance, "I am a bad man. I have had a university education—practiced law for seven years, went wrong and became a tramp, an outcast, the drunken hobo you see. Two days ago I was going to jump into the bay, when this friend, (pointing to a roughly dressed young man) told me of this place and that people got healed here. Now I am here to be healed of this leg, and I know it will be done."

He had been kicked by a horse last May and the bone had healed in a lapped position instead of being joined end to end, leaving him very lame. Well, Bro. Manley and the saints went right back to the chair where the man was sitting, and Bro. Manley prayed the prayer of faith, laying his hands on the man's head. And in a few moments, the man jumped to his feet, looked amazed and said, "It's done! It's done!" threw away his crutch and cane and went all over the tent, walking as good as anybody.

The most profound sensation was produced by this exhibition of the power of God, and nearly everybody was in tears and praising God. Oh what a wonderful God we are serving. The man sought for salvation all the afternoon, and late at night was converted.

Our office at 312 Azusa St. has been almost snowed under by letters, sometimes as many as fifty a day. Many are hungry for the baptism with the Holy Ghost; many want healing for their sick bodies or for friends, and others want salvation. Dear ones, if we have not been able to answer your letters, please take this paper for an answer. If you send in questions, we may answer them in the next paper.

THE APOSTOLIC FAITH
VOL. 1, NO. 6

PENTECOST FALLING
In McKeesport, Pa.

322 Brown Ave., McKeesport, Pa., Feb. 8. —The Holy Ghost has fallen on about a dozen here and they are speaking in tongues and we do not know where the work will stop. There have been two who received their call to China. We praise God for His wonderful grace and power. - S.F. Black.

In Mobile, Al.

Davis Ave. and Ann St., Mobile, Ala., Feb. 1. — After a hard battle in this wicked place, the Lord gave me a tent in answer to prayer. We give God all the glory for victory. Five have been sanctified and three received Pentecost. One brother that has been crippled for years has been healed in his foot and can walk without a stick, and we are expecting a great work of the Lord here soon. - F.W. Williams.

In Spokane, Wa.

Spokane, Wash., Mar. 21. Thank God, the work of the Holy Spirit is reaching into the remotest places of the earth. Upwards of thirty have received their Pentecost right here in Spokane in the past few days, speaking in tongues, writing, and praising God in all things. The Apostolic Light will be somewhat delayed, owing to my removal from Portland office to the work to which God called me in Spokane. - M.L. Ryan.

In Burgess, S.C

Burgess, S.C. March 16. —We are having a wonderful meeting in our midst. Several are being baptized with the Holy Ghost. The people are coming by crowds and God's great work is spreading. Glory to God for this wonderful salvation that is coming back to earth again. - Mc. D. Brown.

In Santa Cruz, Cal.

Pentecost has fallen in Santa Cruz. The last report from there people were getting saved, sanctified, and baptized with the Holy Ghost, and healed. Many seeking. Bro. and Sister T.W. McConnell have been laboring there and Bro. Wilkinson has been assisting.

In Long Beach, Ca.

The Lord is blessing in Long Beach, Cal. We cannot tell just how many at this date have received their Pentecost and speak in tongues. Hungry souls are seeking. The street meetings are attended by crowds. Last Sunday night, many had to be turned away. Bro. McCauley has charge of the work. He says, "The Lord has wonderfully planted the seed of salvation in Long Beach in street meetings every Sunday afternoon. O how I praise Him for the outpouring of His Spirit. A baby that had been sick all its life was wonderfully healed in answer to prayer. Peace be to all the saints in Christ Jesus. Amen." - E. McCauley, Long Beach, Cal.

In Des Moines, Ia.

1624 Oakland Ave., Des Moines, Ia., Feb. 21. — God is working here. Seven or eight are speaking in tongues and others awakened to the truth. I myself have received the gift and speak in many different tongues and can interpret the same. the burden of the Spirit seems to be the blindness of the people, the soon coming of the Lord, the awful judgments that are coming, and to prepare messengers and a bride for His coming. The mission is becoming a center for the hungry ones and too small to accommodate the people. God bless you all. We have had no teaching outside, except our own close walk with God and getting down, down, down before Him and proving Him who never fails. Praise His name. Yours in the rapture, E.C. Ladd.

In San Francisco, Ca.

215 Locust Ave., San Francisco, Cal., Mar. 8. — The Lord is working mightily in San Francisco. Many souls have been converted, sanctified, and baptized with the Holy Ghost and fire,

and healed by the power of God. One Methodist preacher by the name of H.O. Lanham who came to our meetings a few days ago received the baptism with the Holy Ghost Tuesday night (Mar. 5), and spoke in tongues as the Spirit gave utterance. A Baptist preacher who was backslidden got saved, sanctified and baptized with the Holy Ghost and healed, and is now ready to go out and preach the Gospel of Christ in its purity. Bro. Prentiss came to us from Los Angeles and the Lord is blessing him in the meetings. Yours truly in the Lord. — Adolph Rosa.

In San Jose, Ca.

25 Short Ridge Ave., San Jose, Cal., Mar. 4. — Praise God for victory. Thirteen have received their Pentecost and Bible evidence since we came here. Glory to God! The whole place is stirred. Sunday there were eight healed as soon as I anointed them, and they shouted praises to God. Sunday was a hallelujah day all day. Praise God. Sinners are under awful conviction here. The hall is crowded and the people cannot all get in. We are looking for the power to fall as on Pentecost. Yours in Christ, H. McLain.

In Topeka, Kan.

924 N. Kansas Ave., Topeka, Kans., Feb. 21. — Glory to Jesus for the real Pentecostal power that is coming back to His people. About three months ago, Bro. and Sister Batman stopped off here for a few days on their way to Africa, and told of the wonderful work of God going on in the West, and it made us real hungry for more of God, and we began to seek earnestly for the Baptism with the Holy Ghost. Soon afterwards a band of workers came from Denver and were with us ten days. Several

received the baptism while they were here. After they left, we went through some very severe testings, but we held on and when we needed help the worst, God sent Bro. Tom Hezmalhalch and a band of workers to us, for which we praise Him with all our heart. They were with us four weeks and their labors were owned and blessed of God in establishing the work here. A good many were saved and sanctified [sic] and baptized with the Holy Ghost. One young man received his call to the foreign field. We expect the work to move right on. Yours in Jesus, C.E. Foster.

THE APOSTOLIC FAITH
VOL. 1, NO. 11

PENTECOST SPREADS TO OTHER LANDS
Denmark

"Kirkeklokken," a Danish gospel paper, reports that through the Pentecostal outburst in Copenhagen recently, many sinners have come to the Savior, many backsliders have been restored to the joy of salvation, many believers have been filled with the Spirit and have received supernatural gifts.

Wales

Praise God for another brother here who has also now received the Pentecost with tongues. He went home from here speaking in tongues all along the street. There are others to follow. Glory to Jesus. Tonight five or six brothers are coming here for their Pentecost. O, I do praise God that He sent me to Sunderland to get such a wonderful blessing. Praise His holy name. — W. J. Tomlinson, Lynion House, Grove Place, Port Talbot.

Honolulu

Brother and Sister Turney, who have returned from Honolulu, now on their way to Africa report the work in Honolulu: "We had a glorious meeting Honolulu. The power came down and one young man a captain of the Salvation Army, who received his Pentecost, has now opened up an Apostolic Faith Mission in Santa Cruz, Cal. A lieutenant also received his Pentecost and went to carry the news to London, England. Charley Puck, who had a most wonderful experience, is preaching the Gospel on the Island of Hawaii in the city of Kanuela. They are having good meetings and good attendance. People are hungry for the truth."

London, England

I do thank God that there are a few whose eyes God has opened to see their lack and who have waited upon His [Him] in prayer for quite a year and a half at 14, Ackerman Rd., Brixon [sic] S.W., London. God has manifested His almighty power there in the baptism of dear Sister Price and one brother and myself, and I am so glad to send in my testimony to the glory of God and the encouragement of all His children. People are coming from far and near, and no one has been even invited. They just hear how God is working and come. This power was mightily present last Thursday, two sisters being shaken and nearly spoke in tongues. One night the very room was shaken as we read in the Word: "And when they had prayed the place was shaken." Several have had blessed anointings, outpourings of the Spirit and revelations of Jesus Christ. Praise His Holy name.

Mary A. Martin, 319 Southampton St., Camberwell, London, England.

China

Brother and Sister Garr are in Hong Kong, China, last report. God is using them blessedly. A glorious revival is breaking out. Several souls in Hong Kong have received their Pentecost. In Macao and Canton, China, numbers have received the baptism with the Spirit. They are hungry for the Holy Ghost. Brother McIntosh wrote, "They come to our house at all times of the day and rap at our door at 11 and 12 o'clock at night, coming to seek for the Holy Ghost, and we stay up till one and two o'clock praying with them, and glory to God, the Pentecost falls and they speak in tongues." Two sisters who received their Pentecost in Brother Cashwell's work in the South have gone over to help Brother and Sister McIntosh. They are Sister A.E. Kirby and Sister Mabel Evans. Address: Macao, China, care S.C. Todd.

Sweden

Bramaregarden, Hisingstad, Goteborg, Nov. 19. — I am very glad to hear from the old Azusa Mission, my home. I have victory through the dear, cleansing Blood of Christ. Glory to His great name! It is one year today since I came over to Sweden and this city Goteborg. God is still saving, sanctifying, and baptizing with the Holy Ghost, and people are getting healed of God. Last Sunday two got their Pentecostal blessing. We had a wonderful day, the Holy Ghost running the meetings, God's children testifying, praising God, talking in unknown tongues. The fire has begun to fall on small islands near the city. Bless God! The work is still going on in many places in Sweden and God's people are getting more hungry than ever. We trust God to send out more workers into the field. The fire is falling in 'Norrland.' Yet many, many have not heard this Gospel yet. This work will go on till Jesus our Lord comes back. All the saints in Goteborg salute you. Andrew G. Johnson.

Germany

"Auf der Warte," a German paper, says: At Cassel many children of God received the fullness of the Spirit after God had cleansed their hearts by faith. Many children of God have put right old debts. Through the speaking in tongues and the preaching, sins and bonds were revealed, and it was clearly taught that deliverance from the power of sin and the experience of heart cleansing are the conditions for receiving the Pentecostal baptism. The manifestations of the Spirit when the souls were touched were different according to I Cor. 12. Some were knocked down to the floor, some were overflowed gently while sitting in their chairs. Some cried with loud voice, others shouted Hallelujah! clapped their hands, jumped or laughed with joy. Some saw the Lord not only in the meetings, but when silent in the houses, or in bed, or when walking on the road, God touched their souls.

All that was uttered in tongues as far as it concerned salvation was in perfect accord with Scripture. What the Lord gave to utter about His Cross, His Glory, and the Second Coming was refreshment and comfort for every believing soul. Through the speaking of tongues and prophesy [sic] those in the audience received conviction of their sins; which statement is proven by confessions made afterwards to the minister.

The fire is already burning at Grossalmerode. The Lord is doing great things. Many have received the Pentecostal baptism; and the Lord bestowed gifts upon many, especially the gift of tongues and interpretation.

WITNESSES IN ENGLAND

In Britain, the main center in the early Pentecostal period was All Saints Church, near Sunderland, where the Vicar, Alexander Boddy, and his wife, Mary, led conventions designed to provide energy for renewal in the denominations. Boddy had been the secretary of the League of Prayer's center in Monkwearmouth, as well as being a Keswick supporter, but he was to find himself isolated from his former associates, especially after his efforts to circulate a pamphlet, Pentecost for England.

In 1908 Boddy started publishing the first Pentecostal publication, Confidence. A set of 140 issues were published. It was published by Rev. Alexander A. Boddy, of All Saints Church, Monkwearmouth, Sunderland, where in 1907 the Movement commenced in England. The first number is dated April 1908: it was issued monthly till the end of 1916, then bi-monthly, then quarterly, and the last number dated appears to be in 1926. Mr. Boddy traveled in many lands visiting centers of the Movement and Christians from many countries visited Sunderland to experience what God was doing there.

THE FOLLOWING IS TAKEN FROM A REPORT PRINTED IN SUNDERLAND, ENGLAND

Children Receive Pentecost

I was present when the two girls, who were the first children to speak in tongues in England, Janie and May Boddy (the two daughters of the Rev. Alex A. Boddy, All Saints' Vicarage, Sunderland), received their Pentecost. It was at the Vicarage. The nine or ten persons present will never forget the scene. Janie received the interpretation for each sentence, and her childlike simplicity and joy, her beaming face, that I shall never forget, she turned message she received was: "Jesus is coming!" With a surprised look of joy on her face, that I shall never forget, she turned to her mother and kissed her, repeating the words: "Jesus is coming, mother!" Then her fact became serious. She bowed her head a little and lifted her left hand to her cheek (she was kneeling all the time at the end of the table). Again a foreign language was heard. Then came the interpretation: "The Heavens are opened!" followed by the same jubilant glee.

One message was very solemn, spoken, too, with emphasis: "The first shall be last, and the last first." Coming from such childlike lips, it made a great impression on us all. Oh, what joy when she said: "Oh! mummie, Jesus has come, and come to stay; oh, good Jesus, good Jesus!" then peals of joybells of laughter. As she related her experience the next day to a large crowd of children at the Parish Hall, she said, whilst inviting them to seek their Pentecost, "Oh, it is so wonderful, so wonderful!" It was wonderful, it was the Holy Spirit come to dwell within them.

May Boddy had a great revelation of God's power. She prayed so earnestly that she might not "be left out." It was touching, too, to see Janie, who had just received her Pentecost, as she laid her hand on her sister's head and encouraged her: "It's all through the Blood, May, all through the Blood! Jesus is come, He said, May too, May too." May spoke a long time. Some words were very clear. It seemed as if she was constantly claiming Jesus. His name was repeated time upon time. The words, "Aa, Ja, Jesus! Ja, ja, ja, Jesus!" were distinctly Norwegian, with the correct pronunciation (Oh, yes, Jesus! yes, yes, yes, Jesus!) These two dear children have been kind and good girls before and loved Jesus dearly but now they love Him much more and are bold to tell others of His wonderful power to save. T.B. Barratt.

The Apostolic Faith
Vol. 1, No. 12

THE LORD IS SPEAKING IN THE EARTH TODAY

Atlanta, Ga. — The meetings in the hall here have been blessed seasons of refreshing. For six months, every afternoon and night and all day on Sundays, the meetings have continued. Before this "latter rain" such revivals were unheard of. Souls are being saved, sanctified, and healed, and filled with the Holy Ghost. All glory to Jesus' name! Let us follow on to know Him better. This is the beginning of great things.

—"The Bridegroom's Messenger," 53 1/2 Auburn Avenue.

Utica, N.Y. — Blessed be the name of the Lord. Truly these days of the "latter rain" are days of Heaven upon the earth. We are a little band here but full of faith and pressing on. One by one, God is bringing our number into their Pentecost, and is opening other places where there are a few hungry believers longing for their inheritance.

—Birdsell & Mason, 61 State Street.

Strole, Va. — Pentecost has come here. Eight of us are speaking in tongues. We gamblers and drunkards have been saved. Praise the dear Lord. We are looking for dear Jesus every day and can hardly wait to see Him.

—W.S. Woodworth, Caanan Faith Home and Full Gospel Mission.

Portsmouth and Richmond, Va. — Brother Seymour wrote
from these places while he was visiting the missions in the East:
"God is working in Portsmouth. Souls were baptized in
Richmond and God is working in mighty power. The saints are
just as sweet as can be. Glory to God for this Gospel. The saints
are so simple here, that is the reason they receive the Pentecost
so quickly. They are ready for the power."

Philadelphia, Pa. — I have been helping in the Pentecostal
work in one little meeting here. There were a number at the
altar last Sunday and a number were slain under the mighty
power of God. I had a letter from a sister in Danville, Va., a few
days ago, and she says that God is blessing them there and that
souls are being saved, sanctified, and baptized with the Holy
Ghost. Hallelujah! Hallelujah!
—W.M. Scott, 906 Filbert Street, Dec. 4.

Denver, Colo. — Our meetings are being blessed of God. Souls
are being saved, sanctified, baptized with the Holy Ghost and
healed, and the interest is still increasing. All glory be to God
for His wonderful works that He is bestowing upon His children, as He is pouring out His Spirit upon all flesh in these latter days; for the coming of the Lord draweth nigh. The Lord
has held us here and He has opened up an Apostolic Faith
Mission on the corner of Lawrence and Twenty-fourth streets.
The altar is filled with seekers.
—E.S. Lee, 2305 Lawrence Street.

Winnipeg, Canada. —There was a great Pentecostal
Convention in Winnipeg beginning November 15th. Preachers
and workers from all parts of Canada were present. A band of
workers who were in Portland at the time received a call from

God to go to Winnipeg, and they were present at the convention: Sister Crawford and Mildred, Sister Neal, Brother Conlee and Brother Trotter. About twenty were baptized with the Holy Ghost and many were healed. The people brought handkerchiefs and aprons to be blessed as in Acts 19:12, and the Lord did wonderful signs through the simple faith of the dear ones that brought them. The Lord healed one young man of the tobacco habit, taking all the desire for the stuff away from him, through an anointed handkerchief, and he was saved in his own room. Demons were cast out of those bound by them. Our last published report from Winnipeg should have been signed, "The Apostolic Faith Mission, 501 Alexander Ave."

THE APOSTOLIC FAITH
VOL. II, NO. 13

Ireland

Both Belfast and Bangor have been visited with Pentecost.

England

In the past year, news comes that probably 500 people have received the Pentecost in England.

China

We hear from South China that about 100 have received the baptism with the Holy Ghost and they now have a paper in the Chinese called "Pentecostal Truths," which is being scattered in China and Japan. It is a blessed paper and one can feel the power in it even though unable to read it.

West Africa

Brother E. McCauley from Long Beach, California, opened a mission in Monrovia, Liberia. God has been blessing the work. Other missionaries are helping. Sister Harmon writes: "It is marvelous [sic] at times to see the manifestations of the Spirit and to feel the power. They shake like a person with a hard chill; they are in such earnestness when they pray and God does so bless them, until you can hear them a block away."

Jerusalem

One native minister of Beyroute [Beirut], Syria, came to Jerusalem to spend the winter. God has baptized him with the Holy Ghost and he speaks with tongues. Praise God! God started this movement in A.D. 32 in this dear old city, and the "latter rain" is falling in 1908. Glory to God! Miss Elizabeth Brown of the Christian and Missionary Alliance, received her baptism more than two weeks ago. She had the real old fashioned manifestations like many had at Azusa Street. The secret of the matter was she was so given up to God. Praise His name! She came to my room and requested me to lay hands on her for her baptism. She felt waves of fire passing through her head and face and then began to speak in tongues. She sings the heavenly chant. It is precious to hear her. - Lucy M. Leatherman, Jerusalem, Palestine, care of American consulate.

Chapter Seven

WOMEN OF AZUSA

FOR seven days a week, night and day, for over seven years, people from around the city of Los Angeles and around the world gathered together at 312 Azusa Street to experience what God was doing at that former livery stable. The people contended that there was no leader except for the Holy Spirit. Nevertheless, William Seymour played a key role in what God was doing there at the Azusa Mission.

Besides Brother Seymour, the ministry was very dependent on the many women who supported him in the work and who played a key role in the daily schedule there at Azusa. Working with William Seymour at the Azusa Street revival of Los Angeles in 1906 were his wife, Jenny Evans Moore Seymour; Anna Hall, who preached among Armenians and Russians in Los Angeles; and revival leader Lucy Farrow. Many did not like the fact, however, that God was using African-Americans and women in this fresh move of the Spirit. All the same, God kept calling both into the work of the ministry, and women continued to play a strategic role in what was happening in the revival, as well as spreading its message to the rest of the world.

The pastor of William Seymour's church in Houston, before he began attending Charles Parham's Bible School in 1905, was a woman named Lucy Farrow. She was also later associated with Seymour at Azusa Street and conducted her own preaching campaigns in Virginia, Liberia, and other places. Lucy Farrow was described as an "anointed handmaiden" whose ministry included laying on of hands through which seekers received the Pentecostal experience.

It was also a woman, Neely Terry, who invited Seymour to Los Angeles in 1906, where he founded the Azusa Street mission. On his way from Texas to California, Seymour stayed in the headquarters of the Pillar of Fire denomination in Denver which was headed by a woman, Alma White, and

Julia W. Hutchins was pastor of the church to which Seymour was first invited in Los Angeles.

Women in leadership roles at Azusa would eventually include Jenny Evans Moore (who married Seymour in 1908), Mrs. G.W. Evans, Phoebe Sargent, Lucy Farrow, Ophelia Wiley, Clara Lum, and Florence Crawford. Six of the twelve elders at the Azusa Street mission who were in charge of examining potential missionaries and evangelists for ordination were women. Women also led the singing and sometimes preached to the congregation at Azusa. And when Seymour died in 1922, his wife, Jenny, continued as pastor of the Azusa Mission.

Large numbers of women preachers went out from Azusa or, after visiting Azusa, went back to various parts of the world to preach. These included Ivey Campbell, who preached in Ohio; Mabel Smith who "preached nightly to overflowing crowds" in Chicago; Rachel Sizelove in Missouri; Lucy Leatherman, who made a trip around the world; Daisy Batman and Julia Hutchins, who preached in Liberia; and Florence Crawford who carried on the Apostolic Faith Mission in Oregon.

Although there is little information about most of these women, this chapter gives a glimpse into their lives and reveals the influence they had in the work of the Azusa Street Mission. It wasn't just those attending services at Azusa who felt their impact, however; these women took their good works to other cities and countries as well, spreading the word about what God did at Azusa.

One woman who deserves special mention is Neely Terry, the woman who suggested that Julia Hutchins invite William Seymour to her church. In the summer of 1905, Sister Terry went to visit a family in Houston. According to Ethel Goss, Terry worked as a cook in Parham's house.[1] It is believed that Sister Neely also attended Charles Parham's Bible school where she probably met Seymour. More than likely she also met Lucy Farrow, who was working for Parham at that time. In the winter of 1905, Sister Neely returned to Los Angeles where her family had been kicked out of their Baptist church because of their holiness beliefs. Neely's family then helped organize a church at 9th and Santa Fe Street in Los Angeles that was pastored by Julia Hutchins. When the church was looking for male leadership, it was Sister Neely who suggested to her family that they call William Seymour to be the pastor of this new church.

Although Sister Neely receives very little mention in the archives of church history, she played the key role of bridge builder between the work in Los Angeles and William Seymour, who would play a major role in the coming Azusa Revival. We can never minimize any task that one might play in the work of God.

JULIA HUTCHINS

Julia W. Hutchins was the pastor of a Holiness church in Los Angeles, California, which was affiliated with the Church of the Nazarene, founded by Phineas Bresee. This church was formed in the spring of 1905 after Julia and eight African-American families were asked to leave Second Baptist Church of Los Angeles, an African-American church, for "professing holiness doctrine." Julia was the ostracized group's leader.

After their expulsion, the group held effective public services at 214 Bonnie Brae Street, the home of Mr. and Mrs. Richard Asberry. Then they leased a mission hall at 9th and Santa Fe. The church also became a part of the Southern California Holiness Association—primarily an African-American organization.

In the meantime, after a short time attending Parham's Bible Training School, Brother Seymour received a letter from Mrs. Neely Terry, who was living in Los Angeles, California, asking him to consider becoming pastor of a Nazarene group led by Mrs. Julia W. Hutchins. She explained that this was a small black group of about 20 believers who gathered together in worship. Brother Seymour agreed and arrived in Los Angeles on February 22, 1906. Upon arriving, Seymour found the families meeting at 9th and Santa Fe Streets, a facility rented by Hutchins because of the increasing number of participants.

Brother Seymour was well received and often preached on the topics of holiness and divine healing. In March 1906, shortly after arriving, Seymour began to preach about the baptism of the Holy Ghost with the evidence of speaking in other tongues. At the time, he had not yet experienced this baptism himself, but, nevertheless, he preached fervently on the subject, expecting the gift to be released in his newfound church.

However, this new teaching totally shocked the congregation, and Seymour found himself in the middle of an uproar. One Sunday evening, Brother Seymour discovered the door to the church tightly closed and locked with a large silver padlock. A fearful Julia Hutchins had locked out the new pastor, and Seymour was marooned on the street with no place to go. By the grace of God, however, the Lee family, former attendants of the Santa Fe meetings, reached out and gave him a place to stay in their home.

Although the relationship between Sister Hutchins and Brother Seymour did not get off to a very good start, something happened as the Azusa Revival gained momentum. There are several positive and glorious references to Sister Hutchins in *The Apostolic Faith*—Seymour's newspaper that reported Azusa activities. Specifically, in the second issue of the newspaper, there are glowing reports about Sister Hutchins leaving for Africa:

A company of three missionaries left Los Angeles September 13, and are en route for the west coast of Africa. Sister Hutchins has been preaching the Gospel in the power of the Spirit. She has received the Baptism of the Holy Spirit and the gift of the Uganda language, the language of the people to whom she is sent. A brother who has been in that country understands and has interpreted the language she speaks. Her husband is with her and her niece, who also has been given the African language.

On the way to Africa, Hutchins kept a journal of her salvation and then her call to Africa. Evidently, she sent that back to the team at Azusa for it is recorded in that same second issue of *The Apostolic Faith* newspaper:

I was justified on July 4, 1901, and at that time, I felt that the Lord wanted me in Africa, but I was not then at all willing to go. On July 28, 1903, the Lord sanctified me. Before He sanctified me, He asked me if I would go to Africa. I promised Him I would. From that time on, I have felt the call to Africa, and have been willing to go at any moment, but not knowing just when the Lord would have me leave.

On the sixth of last month, while out in my back yard one afternoon, I heard a voice speaking to me these words: "On the 15th day of September, take your husband and baby and start out for Africa." I looked around and about me to see if there was not someone speaking to me, but I did not see anyone, and I soon recognized that it was the voice of God. I looked up into the heavens and said, "Lord, I will obey." Since then, I have had many tests and temptations from the devil. He has at times told me that I would not even live to see September 15, but I never once doubted God. I knew that He was able to bring everything to pass that He told me to do.

After hearing the voice telling me to leave Los Angeles on the 15th, I went to one of my neighbors and testified to her that the Lord had told me to leave for Africa on September 15. She looked at me with a smile. I asked her what she was smiling about. She said, "Because you have not got street car fare to go to Azusa Street Mission tonight, and talking about going to Africa." I told her I was trusting in a God that could bring all things to pass that He wanted us to do. He has really supplied all my needs in every way, for the work where He has called me.

I want to testify also about my husband. He was a backslider, and the devil tested me, saying: "You are going out to cast the devil out of others, and going to take a devil with you." My husband was not saved, but I held on to God and said, "Lord, I will obey."

I continued to testify and to make preparations to leave on the 15th. The Lord reclaimed my husband, sanctified him wholly, and put the glory and the shout in him. Now, it is my time to laugh. The devil has oppressed and mocked me; but praise the Lord, now I can mock him. Glory to God!

It is now ten minutes to four o'clock in the afternoon on the 15th day of September. I am all ready and down to the Mission with my ticket and everything prepared, waiting to have hands laid on and the prayers of the saints, and expect to leave at eight o'clock from the Santa Fe station en route for Africa. We expect to go to Mt. Coffee, Monrovia, Liberia.

Feeling the need of a real companion in the Gospel that was out and out for God, I prayed to God that He might give me one to go with me. I had my eyes upon one that I wanted to go, but in prayer and humility before God, I found out it was not the one the Lord wanted to go. I said, "Anyone, Lord, that you would have to go will be pleasing to me." To my surprise, He gave me my niece, a girl that I had raised from a child. Now she is nineteen years of age, is saved, sanctified and baptized with the Holy Spirit, and is going with me out into the work of the Lord. Therefore, instead of giving me one companion, He gave me two: my niece and my husband.

Our first stop will be Chattanooga, Tennessee, Harge Row. I want the prayers of the saints that I may stay humble.

— Mrs. J.W. Hutchins; Mt. Coffee, Monrovia, Liberia, Africa

In the fifth issue (January 1907) of *The Apostolic Faith* newspaper mention is again made of the team, including Sister Hutchins, after they had just sailed for Africa the latter part of December. In the report back to Azusa, they ask for the prayers of the saints in Los Angeles: "Pray for us, dear ones, as we reach our field of labor. We overcome through the precious Blood. May we all keep humble and filled with the Spirit. We must now say goodbye, but we are not far separated in Christ."

In the seventh issue (April 1907) of *The Apostolic Faith* newspaper, a final reference is made about Sister Hutchins and the missionary team who are in Monrovia actively involved in leading people into the baptism of the Holy Spirit. The message from the team is dated March 26, 1907:

We opened a ten-day meeting in a schoolhouse, and on the tenth night, the Lord came in mighty power. Two were baptized with the Holy Spirit and spoke in tongues. Ten here have received sanctification, and five are filled with the Holy Spirit and speaking in tongues. A brother and his household have been baptized with the Holy Spirit. God has called him to the ministry and he will be baptized Sunday the 30th of March. We have been holding meetings going on three months. The Lord is sending a crowd of the African natives to the meeting and He is working wonderfully with them. The house is filled with the natives every service and they are being saved and sanctified and filled with the Holy Spirit and healed of all manner of diseases. The Lord surely is working with the native Africans of this land. All the saints send love.

LUCY FARROW

Lucy Farrow's integral part in the Azusa Street Revival is evidenced first through her earlier relationship with William Seymour in Houston and then with the support she supplied when arriving in Los Angeles. The first issue of *The Apostolic Faith* newspaper offers a little glimpse into her life:

> From Houston, Texas, to Los Angeles, bringing the Full Gospel. God has greatly used her as she laid hands on many that have received the Pentecost and the gift of tongues. She has now returned to Houston, en route to Norfolk, VA. This is her old home that she left as a girl, being sold into slavery in the south. The Lord she feels is now calling her back. Sister Farrow, Brother WJ Seymour and Brother JA Warren were the three that the Lord sent from Houston as messengers of the Full Gospel.

Farrow was born sometime before 1864 when the slaves were freed because she is said to have "been sold as a child" which means that she was probably between the ages of three/four and ten years old. Estrelda Alexander, in her book, *The Women of Azusa Street*, writes that Farrow was born in Norfolk, Virginia in 1851.[2] This would mean she was 45, plus up to 10 years older, by the time of the Houston revival. Rilda Cole refers to her as "Auntie," a title often used for respected black ladies.[3] She is also referred to as Mrs. Farrow, so she was probably married sometime in the earlier years. There is no indication about how many children she might have had, if any.

While attending the Bryan Hall meetings, Lucy Farrow became friends with the Parham family and was offered the position of governess.

As mentioned in previous chapters, although she was pastor of a small Holiness church, Farrow decided to return to Kansas when the Parhams left Texas. At that time, she had recently become friends with Seymour and asked him to pastor her church until she returned a couple of months later.[4] While in Baxter Springs, in the summer of 1905, she received the baptism of the Holy Spirit, becoming the first black person to come into Pentecost.

We know very little about Farrow, only that she was said to be pastor of the Holiness church in Houston to which Neely Terry came from California to visit and where she met Seymour. Farrow was said to be a musician, and before she left for Los Angeles, she "was engaged as a cook at the school."[5]

Her rise to prominence followed her receiving the baptism of the Holy Spirit. It is usually assumed that through her influence, Seymour came in contact with Parham's teaching, eventually leading him to attend Parham's Bible school.

Seymour went to Los Angeles, arriving February 22, still without experiencing the baptism of the Holy Spirit. During the following weeks, Seymour made a strong pitch to the group to invite Lucy Farrow to come join the work, and money was collected to bring her. Seymour then arranged for Lucy Farrow and A.J. Warren to come to California. When Farrow arrived, Seymour called for ten days of prayer and fasting.

Farrow was staying as a guest in the home of "Irish" Owen Lee, the "Fighting Irishman," a white man who worked as a bank janitor. On April 9, at Lee's request, after much heart searching, she laid her hands on him, and he broke out in tongues. He left immediately for the Bonnie Brae Street prayer meeting at the Asberrys' home, and when he walked through the door with his hands raised, speaking in tongues, the fire fell on those present.

There is some debate whether it was Seymour who laid hands on Lee or if it was Lucy Farrow. It is possible that there were two separate events. According to Emma Cotton, one of the key women during those days at Azusa, it was Sister Farrow who laid hands on him. "Sister Farr[ow] rose from her seat, walked over to Brother Lee and said, 'The Lord tells me to lay hands on you for the Holy Ghost.' And when she laid hands on him, he fell out of his chair, as though dead, and began to speak in other tongues."[6]

The remaining information about Lucy Farrow is spread throughout the various issues of *The Apostolic Faith* newspapers.

When Lucy traveled to Norfolk, Virginia, it was said, "This is her old home which she left as a girl, being sold into slavery in the south." A very brief stop in New Orleans resulted in praying for two people for healing.[7]

In a few weeks, some 159 received the Baptism in Portsmouth. Her attitude was "When the Lord says go, I must go" and she believed He was calling her to Africa. She joined with others in Chicago, and they left for Africa, by way of England, the last of December.[8]

According to a report in issue 12 of *The Apostolic Faith* newspaper, she had arrived in Liberia and sent this report:

Our dear Sister Farrow, who was one of the first to bring Pentecost to Los Angeles, went to Africa and spent seven months at Johnsonville, 25 miles from Monrovia, Liberia, in that most deadly climate. She has now returned and has a wonderful story to tell. Twenty souls received their Pentecost, numbers were saved sanctified and healed. The Lord had given her the gift of the Kru language and she was permitted to preach two sermons to the people in their own tongue. The heathen some of them after receiving the Pentecost, spoke in English and some in other tongues. Praise God. The Lord showed her when she went, the time she was to return and sent her the fare in time, brought her home safely, and used her in Virginia and in the South along the way.

In November 1907, she was back in America conducting services in an Apostolic Faith Mission in Littleton, North Carolina. In May 1908, she was in Los Angeles and we read this report in the final issue of *The Apostolic Faith* newspaper:

> The Lord had baptized a number in the little faith cottage back of the Mission. He has used our dear Sister Farrow from Texas since the beginning of the outpouring of the Spirit in Los Angeles. In her room in the cottage, quite a number have received a greater filling of the Spirit and some have been healed and baptized with the Spirit since she returned from Africa.

According to Estrelda Alexander, she returned to Houston, and within five years she contracted intestinal tuberculosis and died in February 1911.

JENNY MOORE SEYMOUR

Jenny Moore was born in 1884 in Austin, Texas. By 1906, her family had found their way to Los Angeles and were living at 217 Bonnie Brae, just down the street from where the revival took place. The little group continued to gather for prayer and worship, ultimately conducting services in the home of Richard and Ruth Asberry at 214 Bonnie Brae Street. Others learned of the meetings and began to attend, including some white families of nearby holiness churches. On April 9, 1906, a breakthrough occurred as Owen Edward Lee was baptized with the Holy Spirit and began to speak in tongues after Seymour had prayed with him. The two then made their way to the Asberry home. There they had a song, prayers, and testimonies, followed by Seymour's sermon using Acts 2:4 as a text. Following the sermon, Lee raised his hands and began to speak in tongues.

The Spirit of God moved upon those attending, and six others began to speak in tongues that same evening. Jenny Moore, who would later marry William Seymour, was among them. She became the first woman in Los Angeles to receive the baptism in the Holy Spirit. After the experience, she began to sing in tongues and play the piano under the power of God, having never played the piano prior to this occasion. A few days later, on April 12, William Seymour finally received his baptism at about four o'clock in the morning, after having prayed all night long.

Jenny Moore Seymour
(Used by permission. Flower Pentecostal Heritage Center)

In the eighth issue of *The Apostolic Faith* newspaper, she explained the events of that day in an article titled, "Music from Heaven."

It has been often related how the Pentecost fell in Los Angeles over a year ago in a cottage prayer meeting. Sister Jenny Moore who was in that meeting and received her Pentecost gives her testimony as follows:

MUSIC FROM HEAVEN

For years before this wonderful experience came to us, we as a
family, were seeking to know the fullness of God, and He was
filling us with His presence until we could hardly contain the
power. I had never seen a vision in my life, but one day as we
prayed there passed before me three white cards, each with two
names thereon, and but for fear I could have given them, as I
saw every letter distinctly. On April 9, 1906, I was praising the
Lord from the depths of my heart at home, and when the
evening came and we attended the meeting the power of God
fell and I was baptized in the Holy Spirit and fire, with the evidence of speaking in tongues. During the day, I had told the
Father that although I wanted to sing under the power I was
willing to do what ever He willed. At the meeting when the
power came on me, I was reminded of the three cards that had
passed me in the vision months ago. As I thought thereon and
looked to God, it seemed as if a vessel broke within me and
water surged up through my being that when it reached my
mouth came out in a torrent of speech in the languages which
God had given me. I remembered the names of the cards:
French, Spanish, Latin, Greek, Hebrew, Hindu, and as the message came with power, so quick that but few words would have
been recognized, interpretation of each message followed in
English, the name of the language would come to me. I sang
under the power of the Spirit in many languages, the interpretation both words and music which I had never before heard.
In the home where the meeting was being held, the Spirit led
me to the piano, where I played and sang under inspiration,
although I had not learned to play. In these ways God is continuing to use me to His glory ever since that wonderful day,
and I praise Him for the privilege of being a witness for Him
under the Holy Spirit's power.

When the meetings moved to 312 Azusa Street, Sister Moore was actively involved in the worship, leading the singing and playing the piano. She was also a part of the administrative board. She was eventually appointed an evangelist, although she always simply considered herself "a witness for Him under the Holy Spirit's power."

She was also one of the many who went out from the mission traveling to various parts of the United States. The 12th volume of *The Apostolic Faith* newspaper states that she worked in Chicago and other places:

> Sister Jenny E. Moore, who with two other precious sisters from Azusa Mission, Los Angeles, have been working in Chicago and other places, writes: "Truly, beloved, the mission at 943 W. North Avenue is a blessed place, many Spirit-filled men and women and children. They have more children than at Azusa and they are filled. Beloved, I would you could see them."

On May 13, 1908, Seymour married Jenny Evans Moore, a little over two years after the revival began. It is possible that Seymour sensed that there might be a reaction to his marriage. One of the prevailing ideas in the Holiness movement was that the imminent return of the Lord left no room for marriage. In several of *The Apostolic Faith* newspaper articles, Seymour addressed the issue of marriage, possibly to combat these ideas among the Holiness people. In a sermon titled, "The Sermon Tie," he wrote that marriage is "honorable in all" and that "the forbidding of marriage is a doctrine of devils." Secondly, it appears that Clara Lum might have been holding out expectations that Seymour would marry her. There is no way to confirm if this is true; but Lum, who was the secretary for the Azusa Street Mission, was angry when the marriage took place. Clara left Los Angeles and moved to Portland, Oregon, where she joined with minister Florence Crawford.

In the declining years of Azusa, the Seymours served together in directing the work, and when William died in 1923, Jenny carried on the work until three years before her death in 1936.[9]

FLORENCE CRAWFORD

Florence Crawford was probably the most influential woman who helped extend the influence of Azusa beyond the height it experienced in the first few years. Though she was not a part of the original group at Bonnie Brae, Crawford rose quickly to a place of prominence after her encounter with God at 312 Azusa Street.

Crawford, in her own words, was brought up in a home of unbelief, never knowing what it was like to hear her mother pray nor lay her hand on a Bible. It was clear that God had his eye on young Florence and preserved her for His future purposes in her life. Despite poor health, it appears that she had a normal life growing up, enjoying all the social activities that young people participated in, in those days. She describes her first direct encounter with God when she was a teenager:

> One night as I was dancing in a ballroom I heard a voice speak out of Heaven and say "Daughter, give Me thine heart." I did not know it was the voice of God so I went on dancing. Again the voice spoke. It seemed my feet became heavy and the place was no longer beautiful to me. Again the voice spoke much louder, "Daughter, give Me thine heart!" The music died away and I left the ballroom; and for three days and nights I prayed and wept, wrestling against the powers of atheism and darkness. The enemy would tell me there was no God, and that the Bible was a myth. I could hardly eat or sleep, and it seemed there was no hope for me, but I thought: Why did God speak out of Heaven if there were no hope?[10]

In 1890, at the age of 18, she went to Los Angeles and married a building contractor, Frank Crawford. They had two children, and after a shaky start, they eventually separated in 1907. At this time, Crawford embarked on a spiritual journey seeking sanctification through the baptism of the Holy Spirit. She moved from church to church longing to experience God in a deeper and more intimate way.

Her spiritual journey finally took her to 312 Azusa Street where she met a host of "hallelujahs" that went straight through her soul. Feeling that she had found her home, her own poignant words describe that day and the wonderful joy that filled her heart.

> How I thank God that when I heard of the outpouring of the Holy Ghost, He led me to a little mission. It was not a fine hall, but just an old barn-like building with an old board laid on two chairs for an altar. The floor was carpeted with sawdust; the walls and beams blackened by smoke. I looked around to see if anybody saw me go in, but I would not have cared if the whole world saw me go out. I had found a people who had the experience I wanted. The first "Hallelujah" I heard echoed down in my soul. When I went out of there that day, the only thing I wondered was: Can I ever get it?[11]

Soon after, she received the baptism in the Holy Spirit and was water baptized. Her gift quickly made room for her among the leadership at Azusa, and eventually she became one of the six members of the administrative board. It was not long after that when Crawford and Clara Lum started recording all the events of the revival and with Seymour launched the first issue of *The Apostolic Faith* newspaper.

Throughout the 13 issues of the newspaper, exploits of Sister Crawford were shared. The first news we read about concerns the great work that she was a part of in the city of Oakland. Recorded in the first and third issues of the newspaper:

FIRE FALLING AT OAKLAND

A band of workers left Los Angeles for Oakland. All are baptized with the Holy Spirit and speak in tongues. They are Brother GW Evans and wife, Sister Crawford, Brother Johnson, Louise Condit and Brother Manley, editor of the Household of God. Brother Manley had come down from Oakland especially to see the movement but did not receive his Pentecost until after he returned. Reports brought back by Brother Evans are that hundreds have been at the altar, many converted, sanctified, and healed, and thirty have received their Pentecost and are speaking in tongues. Praise God! The saints of Los Angeles rejoice to hear the good report.[12]

The second issue of the newspaper reported that, "In the City of Oakland, during the five weeks that the band from Los Angeles was there, Brother and Sister Evans and Sister Florence Crawford, sixty-five souls received the Baptism of the Holy Spirit, and thirty were sanctified and nineteen converted."

Even though a great revival was breaking out in Oakland, Sister Crawford had a huge tug on her heart, drawing her north to Oregon. She loved what God was doing in Los Angeles and she understood that the work there was something very special, but the cry of souls was calling her to other places as she describes in the second issue: There is no spot on earth so dear to me as this place, but I must go out and tell this story. Souls are perishing far and near. The Lord told me yesterday to go into the entire world and preach His Gospel. "The kingdom of heaven is at hand," and "Behold, I come quickly." What He says to me, He says to every baptized soul. He wants us to go out into the highways and hedges and declare this Gospel. He has anointed me to tell the story of Jesus and I can go alone for Jesus is with me. Oh, glory to God!

On December 25, 1906, Sister Crawford arrived in Portland, the city that would become her home and the base for the Apostolic Faith

Mission in the Northwest. She did not waste any time. A few days later, she writes this testimony in the fifth issue of the paper:

APOSTOLIC FAITH MISSION IN PORTLAND

The power fell before the meeting was half through and two received Pentecost at night, two more. Last night Mildred received her Pentecost. The slain of the Lord lay so you can't move about the altar. The altar is full before the meeting is half over. The house is just packed. Oh, if we only had a larger hall. I cannot tell how God is working here.

In a letter dated a week later, she again told how the crowds were crowding into the hall. Every chair was filled, the aisles packed, the doorway jammed, and crowds stood out in the street. When an invitation to prayer was given, there were so many who wanted to pray that it was difficult to find room at the altar or elsewhere.

On January 8, her initial trip concluded, Sister Crawford returned to Los Angeles. However, by the following April, she was on her way back to Portland. The pastor of the group which met in the old converted blacksmith shop had contacted the owners of property at 12th and Division Street in Portland, wanting to make arrangements to hold a camp meeting there. The owners were initially reluctant, saying that the "tongues of fire" might set the woods ablaze, but they finally consented to let them use the location. After the camp meeting, the Portland congregation moved to a hall on Southwest First and Madison, for they were greatly in need of a larger place of worship. As the Lord continued to bless, the pastor offered to turn his church over to Florence Crawford. It would be her church—the Apostolic Faith Church of Portland, Oregon. During a Gospel outreach trip to Minneapolis, God spoke to her, saying, "If you will go back to Portland, Oregon, and stay there, I will make that place the headquarters of the Apostolic Faith work, and I will raise up the standard of the Gospel in that city."

God's plan was unmistakable, and in 1908 Florence Crawford gave up her home in Los Angeles and moved to Portland. According to Crawford, the Azusa Street ministry turned over the responsibility of publishing *The Apostolic Faith* newspaper to her, so she and her cowork-er, Clara Lum, moved to Portland bringing with them the coveted mailing list for *The Apostolic Faith* newspaper.

Controversy Over the Mailing List

Because Seymour no longer had a copy of his mailing list, which was also his list of supporters from all over the United States and the world, and especially those in the Midwest, he was no longer able to publish the newspaper. There are those who say that it was stolen by Crawford and Lum. However, the Portland Apostolic Faith Mission has replied to this accusation by saying that Crawford and Lum took only two lists, leaving twenty other copies of the list with Seymour.

Douglas Nelson writes in his book, *For Such A Time As This: The Story of Bishop William J. Seymour and the Azusa Revival*[13], that Clara Lum stole the international mailing lists and fled to Portland, Oregon. There she joined with Florence Crawford in ministry. Many others hold to this position of Nelson's and see this as the beginning of the end of the revival in Los Angeles.[14]

To be fair, it is important to report the position of those who are a part of the Apostolic Faith Mission that still exists in Portland, Oregon. In response to Nelson's position, they have responded with the following defense:

Evidence of the fact that she brought the publishing work to Portland with the blessing of the Azusa Street ministry is the fact that the first edition of the 13th issue of *The Apostolic Faith* paper which was published in Los Angeles in May 1908, (after Florence Crawford moved to Portland) contained this note: "For the next issue of this paper address The Apostolic Faith Campmeeting, Portland, Oregon." It also refers to Florence Crawford as "Sister Crawford" and mentions her activities in Portland. At that juncture, publishing of the paper was transferred to Florence Crawford's headquarters in Portland. It is our understanding that only two of the twenty-two complete mailing lists were brought to Portland. She continued the publishing of The Apostolic Faith paper without interruption, the first edition from Portland coming out in July-August, 1908.

The problem with this explanation is that there is only one reference to Sister Crawford in the 13th issue under the title, "Electric Messages from the Field," which were 10 short messages written by F.L.C. This is most certainly a reference to Sister Crawford, but there is no reference to the address change.

A representative of the Portland Apostolic Faith Mission wrote that the publication of The Apostolic Faith newspaper continued uninterrupted, with the final edition from Los Angeles printed in June 1908. Indeed, there was a 13th and final edition, marked that it was from Los Angeles, and dated May 1908. Writing nothing specific about any other editions of the 13th issue, a representative of the Apostolic Faith Mission in Portland explained (as noted in the quote above). The first edition of the 13th issue of The Apostolic Faith paper which was published in Los Angeles in May 1908, (after Florence Crawford moved to Portland) contained this note: 'For the next issue of this paper address The Apostolic Faith Campmeeting [sic], Portland, Oregon.' It also refers to Florence Crawford as 'Sister Crawford' and mentions her activities in Portland."

Such a notation does appear on the second page of that paper; however, another edition of the 13th issue apparently came out in July-August, 1908, from Portland.

As already mentioned, in the 13th edition, you will not find the words "Sister Crawford," Crawford's name, or a mention of the Portland work. The only reference to Sister Crawford is the aforementioned messages by "F.L.C."

Sister Crawford continued to minister in Portland until her death in 1936. Despite the controversy over the mailing list, no one can deny the passion that Sister Crawford had for Christ, as eloquently exemplified with her passionate words in the 9th issue of *The Apostolic Faith* newspaper.

I can't forget how, kneeling at the dear old board in Azusa Street, I promised God I would go where He wanted me to go and stay where He wanted me to stay, and be what He wanted me to be. I meant every word of it and God has taken me at my Word. How His glory is flooding my soul. Oh, how I worship His precious name! I have to stop and wonder how God can bless the Word through me. To think He has saved me when all my family were infidels and everything that would drive me from God. No one can ever know how I feel for the way God has dealt with me. Oh, how I love Jesus. It thrills my very being to think of the Blood. It has done so much for me. I am filled with wonder love, and praise that God would permit me to see the workings of His mighty power in these last days. Oh, to think we have lived to see the return of the apostolic power and to see the gifts restored back to the church. I find we cannot compromise with anything or anybody. Oh, we must stand for all the light we have received, and having down all to stand.

LUCY LEATHERMAN

Lucy Leatherman was one of the greatest missionaries that went out from the Azusa Street mission. Unfortunately, we know very little about her, but we do know that this dedicated saint of God traveled the most and the farthest than any of those who went out from the little band at Azusa Street. "She endured incredible hardship, going by primitive means to remote locations. Lucy was fully engaged in the culture of the societies to which she ministered, often dressing in native clothing. She exposed herself to the rigors of extreme weather and comparatively uncomfortable accommodations along with the possibility of violence at the hands of robbers that terrorized the surrounding terrain."[15]

In the fourth issue of *The Apostolic Faith* newspaper (Dec. 1906), Sister Lucy, writing from New York City, described her experience at Azusa in these touching words: While seeking for the Baptism of the Holy Spirit in Los Angeles, after Sister Ferrell laid hands on me, I praised and praised God and saw my Savior in the heavens. As I praised, I came closer and closer, and I became so small. By and by, I swept into the wound in His side, and He was not only in me but I in Him, and there I found that rest that passeth all understanding and He said to me, you are in the bosom of the Father. He said I was clothed upon and in the secret place of the Most High. I said, "Father, I want the gift of the Holy Spirit," and the heavens opened and I was overshadowed, and such power came upon me and went through me. He said, Praise Me, and when I did, angels came and ministered unto me. I was passive in His hands, and by the eye of faith I saw angel hands working on my vocal cords, and I realized they were loosing me. I began to praise Him in an unknown language.

In a few days, while on my way to church, I met a woman and two little children. She was talking to her children in a language that sounded like the Words God had given me. I spoke a sentence to her, and she said, "What you say means God has given Himself to you." She is from Beirut, Syria, and speaks Arabic. Eight years ago, in AB Simpson's missionary school at Nyack, New York, I heard the Macedonian cry to go to Jerusalem, but it is to the Arabs. I am told there are more Arabs than Jews there, and God has been speaking to me and asks me if I would be willing to go with Him to the wild Arab of the desert. Anywhere with Jesus I will gladly go.

On land or sea, what matter where,

Where Jesus is 'tis heaven there.

Pray that God will send a revival to this city and pray for Arabia.

Pray for Arabia.

The Spirit of God had already touched her heart motivating her to go to a world where others would not go.

On August 10, 1906, Lucy left Oakland with Brother Andrew Johnson and Sister Louise Condit. As they traveled across the United States to catch a ship in New York City and head for Jerusalem, they stopped in Colorado Springs where four people were baptized in the Spirit, and while in Denver, three more were baptized in the Spirit.

According to their testimony in the Azusa papers, Brother Johnson had received seven different languages, one of which was the Arabic, and Sister Leatherman was able to speak in the Turkish language. In fact, while they were in Oakland, a man wearing the Turkish fez came by. He listened in wonder and asked what college she had attended. He was an educated man from a Turkish college in Constantinople and said that she spoke as perfect a Turkish tongue as he had ever heard spoken by a foreigner. She told him the Holy Spirit gave her the language and that she did not understand herself; he was the first person who had interpreted for her.

Finally reaching New York City, Sister Lucy wrote these words: "Praise God for the gift of the Holy Spirit, the third person in the trinity. We have been receiving letters from those who have been much blessed and have been led into the Pentecost through our sister and the rest of the Palestine Missionary band." (*Apostolic Faith* Vol. 1, No. 2.)

Also, while she was in New York City, Lucy became involved in a prayer meeting with Maud Williams. One of the people invited to those meetings happened to be T.B. Barratt who was a Methodist-Episcopal minister in charge of mission work in Norway and Sweden. In the Azusa papers, Barratt described the meeting that changed his life:Sister Maud Williams who got the blessing in Ontario, Canada and has the gift of tongues, laid her hands on my head and after that I had no more strength in me, although I am physically very strong now. I lay on the floor by the platform in a reclining position. At about half past twelve I asked a brother there and Sister Leatherman to lay their hands on my head again. Just then she says she saw a crown of fire and cloven tongues over my head. The brother saw a supernatural light.

> Immediately I was filled with light and such a power that I began to shout as loud as I could in a foreign language. Between that and four o'clock in the morning I must have spoken seven or eight languages, to judge from the various sounds and forms of speech used. I stood erect at times preaching in one foreign tongue after another, and I know from the strength of my voice that 10,000 might easily have heard all I said. Nine persons remained until three o'clock and are witnesses of the whole scene. The most wonderful moment though was when I burst into a beautiful baritone solo, using one of the most pure and delightful languages I have ever heard. The tune and words were entirely new to me, and the rhythm and cadence of the verses and chorus seemed to be perfect. I sang several times later on. Some of the languages spoken produced a nasal sound and some a deep guttural sound. Oh it was wonderful. Glory! Hallelujah! (*Apostolic Faith* Vol. 1, No. 2.)

In the final issue of the Azusa papers, we read the last report given by Sister Lucy. She had finally reached Jerusalem and was rejoicing with the Pentecostal work that God was doing in that city.

One native minister of Beirut, Syria, came to Jerusalem to spend the winter. God has baptized him with the Holy Spirit and he speaks with tongues. Praise God! God started this movement in 32 AD in this dear old city, and the "latter rain" is falling in 1908. Glory to God! Miss Elizabeth Brown of the Christian and Missionary Alliance, received her baptism more than two weeks ago. She had the real old-fashioned manifestations like many had at Azusa Street. The secret of the matter was she was so given up to God. Praise His name! She came to my room and requested me to lay hands on her for her baptism. She felt waves of fire passing through her head and face and then began to speak in tongues. She sings the heavenly chant. It is precious to hear her.

—Lucy M. Leatherman, Jerusalem, Palestine, care of American consulate.

Leatherman's missionary journeys were spread out over a period of 17 years, beginning in 1906. She finally returned home from Argentina in 1923, after having touched four continents and over ten countries. The trail of her life ends at this point, but her life had already impacted thousands along the way.

ANNA HALL

Another woman who played a very important role, even though we know little about her, was Mrs. Anna Hall. She appears on the scene already baptized in the Holy Spirit and a seasoned preacher. Anna Hall was very close to the Tuthills who had become converted under Parham's ministry. Sometime in 1904, she, with the Tuthills as helpers, conducted a meeting in Lawrence, Kansas. Then in early 1905, in Joplin, she teamed up with a couple called the Oylers who had received the baptism of the Holy Spirit under Parham. From Joplin, they went to Orchard. When Parham arrived in Orchard a few weeks later, she was ready to share the revival duties with him. It was in her home, which she must have established very quickly, that the first Texans received the Baptism. Parham described one service where "Sister Hall and I gave them a rousing talk on victory."[16]

During the month of April she preached on Sundays, both morning and evening, at the local Community Church and shared the pulpit with Parham. She was active in many of the revivals and often shared the pulpit with Parham.[17]

"A letter from Seymour to Parham, Aug. 27, 1906 stated, 'Sister Hall has arrived, and is planning out a great revival in this city, that will take place when you come.' The big meeting, of course was not to be, but Hall, as well as the Oylers and Quintons shared in the YMCA meeting after Parham was excluded from Azusa Mission."[18]

According to some reports, the last time we hear of Sister Hall was that she had gone down among the Catholics, the French Arcadians, and among fisherman, on the coast of Texas, and for two weeks slept on the floor with a pair of blankets under her; and scores of them were saved through hearing her speak in their language.

The curtain closes and there is no mention of her again. Through the following messages from the Azusa papers, we gain a sense of her spiritual insight and passion for God. (*Apostolic Faith* Vol. 1, No. 2.)

THE POLISHING PROCESS

Several years ago, when I was very hungry, seeking God in all His fullness, I shut myself away in my closet one day, and the Lord gave me a wonderful revelation. As I was kneeling before my Maker, beseeching Him to show me all He expected me to be, right before my eyes I saw this wonderful vision. There appeared a man with a large, long, knotty, but straight log. The man had an axe. Did you ever see anybody score timber? He was scoring the log, and it seemed to me that the axe went clear to the bit. Every time he scored, it hurt me. He scored it on four sides and then took the broad axe and whacked off the knots. Then he took a line and with an adz, he made it smooth. Then he raised it in the air and taking a great plane, turned to me and said, "This is the plane of the Holy Spirit." He ran the plane up and down, until I could see the image of the man perfectly reflected in the face of the log, as in a mirror. He did this to all four sides. Then turning to me, he said, "Thou art all fair, my love; there is no spot in thee."

That is what God wants to do with us. He wants to take all the bumps, all the barnacles off. We have only begun to lay ourselves on the anvil of God's truth. The hammer is being applied to us. He may have to throw us back in the smelter several times. Let us stay in the fire until there is no more dross in us. Sometimes we think God has done all He needs to do; but something comes up that we do not like, and the old man can get up and hobble off on a good shin.

Several weeks ago, I thought surely the last stroke is put in, and now I am dead to the world. However, it was not very long until I found out there was a little self there. I was holding a meeting in a little village. We had to move a kitchen stove, and there was no way but for me to get on top of that cook stove and ride behind an old mule team, and I found Sister Hall had a little life in her yet. Thank God, I am dead to that thing now.

Let us stay on the anvil of God, until we reflect the image of the Master. There is a place where God Almighty will say: "Thou art all fair, my love, there is no spot in thee."

—Mrs. Anna Hall

HONOR THE HOLY SPIRIT

Let me warn you, dear ones, as a mother in Israel, Don't try to prune one another. Jesus says: "I am the vine and my Father is the husbandman. Every branch in me that beareth not fruit, he purgeth it." Let Him do the pruning and purging. If you see a brother or sister doing anything you do not approve of, instead of blazing it abroad, get down on your knees and say: "My Father, I honor you to bring them out of this fault." Multitudes and great bodies of Christians have gone to the wall for that very same thing. They tried to prune one another, tried to make others believe just as they believed and think just as they thought. If this movement stands for anything, it stands for unity of mind. It was raised up to answer the prayer of Jesus: "That they might be one, as thou Father art in me and I in thee." What is the matter with the world today? Here is a little selfish sect and it is a denomination by itself. They do not love one another, as God would have them. Let us honor every bit of God there is in one another. Let us honor the Holy Spirit to teach men to get them out of their error. Dear ones watch and pray that ye enter not into temptation. Watch that something does not come in to grieve the Holy Spirit. "Grieve not the Holy Spirit of God whereby ye are sealed unto the day of redemption."

—Mrs. Anna Hall

Harvard College historian Harvey Cox expresses the key role that women played in public meetings at Azusa:

...in the songs and prayers, the sermons and testimonies...the most fundamental revolution is going on because what is being altered is nothing short of what might be called "the gender of God"....The result is...a different God, because those qualities include distinctive feminine ones. The distant jealous and judgmental God of some traditional...theology gives way to a Jesus who longs to embrace sinners, to enter into their hearts in what Cucchiari aptly calls a "soteriological romance." God courts human beings, and is broken hearted when men and women resist His gentle advances. For Pentecostals God is more lover than judge, more concerned with human affection than commanding obedience and is sympathetic with "the murky emotions of the heart."[19]

It is clear even from the casual observer that women from many parts of the country played a key role in the events surrounding the revival at Azusa Street. They were instrumental in bringing Seymour to Los Angeles and helped established the work in the early days.

They came looking for power—the power of the Holy Spirit—and when that power fell, it changed their lives forever. They came looking for a place where they could serve God without restraint and without condemnation. The fire that fell upon their lives empowered them to take the message of Pentecost across the United States and to other countries of the world. They were certainly women of whom the world was not worthy and who set the stage for the many women ministers of the Gospel who would follow them.

ENDNOTES

1. Ethel Goss, *The Winds of God* (New York: Comet Press, 1958), 70.

2. Estrelda Alexander, *The Women of Azusa Street* (Cleveland, OH: The Pilgrim Press, 2005), 39.

3. Sarah Parham, *Life of Charles F. Parham founder of the Apostolic Faith Movement* (Joplin, Mo: Tri-State Printers, reprint 1977, originally published 1930), 120.

4. Liardon, *God's Generals*, 142.

5. http://www.unitypublishing.com/NewReligiousMovements/WhatSpirt8.html

6. Estrelda Alexander, *The Women of Azusa*, 43.

7. *The Apostolic Faith* newspaper, Issue 2, 10/06 p.3, col.2

8. *The Apostolic Faith* newspaper, Issue 4, 12/06, p.1, col. 3

9. Alexander, *The Women of Azusa*, 161.

10. Florence Crawford, *The Light of Life Brought Triumph: A Brief Sketch of the Life and Labors of Florence L. Crawford* (Portland: Apostolic Faith Publishing, 1955), 3-4.

11. http://www.apostolicfaith.org/foryou/articles/fcrawford.asp

12. *The Apostolic Faith* newspaper, issue 1.

13. Ph.D. dissertation, University of Birmingham, England, 1981.

14. http://dunamai.com/Azusa/azusa_pages/History.htm

15. Alexander, *The Women of Azusa Street*, 72.

16. Sarah Parham, *Life of Charles F. Parham*, 108.

17. Stanley Frodsham, *With Signs Following* (Springfield, MO: Gospel Publishing House, originally published 1926), 26.

18. http://www.stbi.edu/cfp_houston_conn.html

19. Harvey Cox, *Fire from Heaven*, p. 200.

Chapter Eight

THE INSIDE STORY OF THE AZUSA STREET OUTPOURING

By Emma Cotton[1]

BROTHER W.J. Seymour, the one whom God used to bring the message that stirred the world, was born in Louisiana. He was saved and sanctified under the "Evening Light Saints," a Holiness group. Later, he came to Houston, Texas, where he met Sister Farrar [Farrow], who had a small Holiness mission. She was led to go to Kansas to attend Bible School and Brother Seymour, who was now one of the congregation, was asked to act as pastor during her absence.

While away Sister Farrar [Farrow], received the light on Acts 2:4. She began to seek for more of God and the Spirit came upon her so strongly that she was unable to remain at Bible School. She then returned to Houston to tell the story of her wonderful new experience.

Before she left for Houston, she heard of a group of Nazarene colored saints in Los Angeles who had organized a little Holiness church on Santa Fe Avenue. Sister Terry (Neely Terry) went to these meetings where she met the pastor, Julia Hutchins. Consequently, when Sister Terry finally arrived in Houston that summer to visit her folks, she visited the Holiness mission there, where she met Brother Seymour.

Sister Terry later returned to Los Angeles where she immediately went out on Santa Fe to the little Nazarene group, and told Sister Hutchins about the "very godly man" she had met in Houston. Right away interest was stirred and the group invited the Holiness preacher, Brother Seymour, to their little church.

Emma Cotton with her husband
(Used by permission, Flower Pentecostal Heritage Center)

Just before Brother Seymour received this invitation to the Coast Sister Farrar [Farrow] had returned from Kansas to her little mission, with her new experience. As she made it known to the preacher, that she had received the Baptism with the Holy Ghost, he was amazed because he had thought the Baptism of the Holy Ghost was received when one was sanctified.

He then began to seek the Lord through prayer and the Word of God. It was then the Lord, in His faithfulness to Brother Seymour, as He is faithful to everyone who is honest, began to show him that he was mistaken about being baptised [sic] with the Holy Spirit; that he was only sanctified.

Brother Seymour began asking the Lord to empty him of his false ideas, and when he was emptied of every false thought and idea that he had, the Lord then made plain to him Acts 2:4, as a personal experience.

By this time, the fare from Los Angeles had reached him, and when he arrived here, he found the saints waiting for him with eagerness to see the man of God of whom they had heard.

Everybody was happy to see him, but on Sunday morning, when Brother Seymour preached on Acts 2:4, as a personal experience, oh! what a surprise to those old saints who had claimed the baptism of the Holy Ghost for years. There they were told by the preacher they did not have the Holy Ghost; they were only sanctified.

When the meeting was dismissed, Brother Lee, a precious colored saint who was a member of the Peniel mission, invited Brother Seymour to his home to dinner. When they returned to the mission to the afternoon service, the lock was on the door, because the saints thought he had a false doctrine, and they would not permit him in the mission any more. So then, Brother Lee, out of courtesy for the stranger, (not that he believed he was right) had to take him back to his home. He could not leave the stranger in the street.

Brother Seymour had no money to get out of town and the saints did not believe in him and he did not know anybody, so he stayed in his room and prayed. Brother and Sister Lee did not feel so good toward him, but they just could not invite him to leave. They had the unwelcome guest on their hands.

After a few nights in the home, Brother Seymour asked them if they would pray when Brother Lee would come in from his work, so they did. In a few nights, the Spirit of God began to take hold of the hearts of Brother and Sister Lee, for prayer, and they felt differently toward the stranger. Then, in a few days more, the saints from the little mission began to come around to see if the stranger was still in town or had gone.

They found such a wonderful spirit of prayer in that home, that they began to humble themselves before the Lord. It was then the Lord began to talk to them and everyone that came into that home would get down and pray. The news began to spread among the people about that praying man. They would not receive his doctrine, but they would pray with him.

Then came a neighbor into the home, a Baptist sister, Sister Asbury of 214 North Bonnie Brae, and invited the stranger, Brother Seymour, to hold the prayer meeting in her home. So they began the prayer meeting in Brother and Sister Asbury's home, and they tarried day and night. In the meantime, the Spirit of the Lord had taken hold of Brother Lee's heart in such a way that he now was in constant prayer. He was a janitor in the bank at Seventh and Spring for years and he said he used to go down into the basement of the bank and hide away and spend hours and hours in prayer.

One day the Lord gave him a vision. He plainly saw two men come to him; apparently Peter and John. He said he was not asleep; he was praying. They stood and looked at him; then they lifted their hands to heaven and they began to shake under the power of God and began to speak in other tongues. And he said he jumped up and he was just shaking, under the power of God, and did not know what was the matter with him. When he went home that night he said to Brother Seymour, "I know now how people act when they get the Holy Ghost." Brother Seymour had explained the manifestation of the Spirit to the group.

This sounded so foolish to them, and Brother Seymour could not explain it enough for them to understand; they just had to get it. After he had this vision, a deeper hunger was stirred in his heart. Brother Seymour could not impress the people, but after Brother Lee had the vision, they began to believe it was a real experience. The Lord created such a hunger in Brother Lee that he began to seek more earnestly for that experience.

One evening he came in from his work, and he said to Brother Seymour, "If you will lay your hands on me, I will receive my baptism." And Brother Seymour said, "No, the Lord wants me to lay hands suddenly on no man." Later on in the evening, Brother Seymour said to Brother Lee, "Brother, I lay my hands on you in Jesus' name," and when he laid his hands on him Brother Lee fell under "the power, like dead, and Sister Lee was so frightened that she screamed and said, "What did you do to my husband?"

In a few minutes, Brother Lee rose up and sat in a chair. Brother Seymour said afterwards that he prayed and asked the Lord to let him get right up as they all seemed so frightened that the Lord could not finish the work at that time. Brother Lee had an heavenly touch then and he sought the Lord day and night.

Brother Seymour told about Sister Farrar [Farrow], whom he had met in Texas, who had given him the light on Acts 2:4, so after Brother Lee has this experience with the Lord, they were anxious to see the woman who had had this wonderful experience in the Holy Ghost, and they got together the money and sent for her.

When Brother Lee came home one evening, and found Sister Farrar [Farrow] there, he fell on his knees at her feet, and he said, "Sister, if you will lay your hands on me, I believe I will get my baptism right now." And she said "I cannot do it, unless the Lord says so."

Later, while at a dinner, Sister Farrar [Farrow] rose from her seat and she walked over to Brother Lee and said, "The Lord tells me to lay my hands on you for the Holy Ghost." And when she laid her hands on him, he fell out of his chair like dead, and began to speak in other tongues. It was so strange to Sister Lee and her brother, that the Lord did not do much through Brother Lee; he just spoke in tongues a few minutes and got up.

They went on over to the prayer meeting at Sister Asbury's home. When Brother Lee walked into the house, six people were already on their knees praying. As he walked in the door, he lifted his hands and began to speak in tongues and the Power fell on them and all six of them began to speak in tongues. Then came the great noise that was spread abroad.

They shouted three days and nights. The people came from everywhere. By the next morning, there was no way of getting nearer the house. As the people came in they would fall under the Power; and the whole city was stirred. They shouted there until the foundation of the house gave way, but no one was hurt. During those three days, there were many people who received their baptism, who had just come to see what it was. The sick were healed, and sinners were saved just as they came in.

Then they went out to find another meeting place, and they found Old Azusa. It was an old discarded building on Azusa Street that had been used for a Methodist church but had been vacant for years. It seemed to have been waiting for the Lord and there began that great world-wide revival, where the people came from all over the world by the hundreds and thousands. That meeting lasted for three years, day and night, without a break.

While I write this, my soul is lifted up, because I saw the house in its first glory and when I remember those days, I feel like going down into the dust of humility, if only to bring back that old-time Power, I am willing to give my life.

I feel that this is the time now for the refreshing of the saints. This old-time Azusa work stood for and still stands for "the earnestly contending for the faith once delivered to the saints." This message of the Lord is a great getting together, that we all might be renewed in the old-time Spirit and Power; that we might do a greater work for Jesus in this last hour.

The noise of the great outpouring of the Spirit drew me, and I had been nothing but a walking drug store all my life, with weak lungs and cancer. As they looked on me, they said, "Child, God will heal you." In those days of that great outpouring, when they said God would heal you, you were healed.

For thirty-three years, I have never gone back to the doctors, thank God, nor any of that old medicine! The Lord saved me, baptized me with the Holy Ghost and healed me, and sent me on my way rejoicing. This is what I saw and heard. I have much more to say about the wonderful working of the Power of God among the people next time, if it is the Lord's will.

(Signed) Mother Cotton

Every conversion is planned in Heaven. "I can no more convert a soul than I can create a star," and angels are our colleagues, carrying forward God's work, not ours.

ENDNOTE

1. Used by permission, Flower Pentecostal Heritage Center.

Chapter Nine

OPPOSITIONS, DIVISIONS, AND CONTROVERSIES

IN John 17:22, Jesus prayed this prayer to the Father, *"I have given them the glory that You gave Me, that they may be one as We are one."* By manifesting His glory in the earth, Jesus' ultimate desire was that this glorious manifestation would cause His people to come into unity. In the history of revival, we see that there is always an initial sense of oneness that breaks out among God's people as, in the early days, His glory is manifested and His name is exalted.

But unfortunately, in every revival, this unity usually degenerates into divisions and fragments into sects. Camelot does not last forever, and so this mighty work of God that began at 312 Azusa Street saw its first chink in the armor as early as 1907. The causes of these fractures are many fold, and this chapter includes an outline of these divisions and controversies with a hope that future generations will learn from their experiences.

One of the obvious problems is that no one, single, long-term leader emerged who consolidated the movement into a cohesive whole, enabling it to avoid potential disintegration. There was no Martin Luther or John Wesley to bring it together. It wasn't because there was no strong, distinct leader, for in the early days Seymour had clearly seen Parham as a spiritual father. In fact, it was Seymour's desire that Parham come and give his blessings to what God was doing in Los Angeles.

We find on the first page of the first issue of *The Apostolic Faith*, a clear indication of Seymour's feelings toward Parham: "Bro. Parham, who is God's leader in the Apostolic Faith Movement." The second edition mentions that the initial evidence of the baptism of the Holy Spirit came in Topeka, Kansas, in 1901 under the leadership of Charles Parham. Unfortunately, this leadership lasted only until Parham actually arrived at the Azusa revival. Sensitive to the growing criticism of hyper-emotionalism in the movement, Parham was appalled by what he saw at Azusa and harshly criticized the frenzied state of those overcome by such intense emotionalism at the altar. When he was asked to leave and eventually barred from the meetings, he became even more vocal in his criticisms. Parham accused the congregation of being under the influence of hypnotists and spiritualists. In one of many interviews, he made this observation:

> I sat on the platform in Azusa Street Mission, and saw manifestations of the flesh, spiritualistic controls, saw people practicing hypnotism at the alter [sic] over candidates seeking the baptism.[1]

Parham moved to another part of town and tried to start a competing work, but he was not very successful, which served to increase the string of callous and cruel comments he made. He went on to claim that Seymour was possessed of a spirit of leadership. Eventually, Parham left Los Angeles repulsed by what he saw and continued to distance himself from the work at Azusa.

Seymour was set on maintaining God as the leader of the work. Again in the first issue of the Azusa paper, we see this commitment: "No church or organization is back of it. All who are in touch with God realize as soon as they enter the meetings that the Holy Spirit is the leader." It is clear that Seymour was the anointed leader of this work, but because he was black, it is possible that his leadership was rejected. In the early days of the revival, we also see a migration away from Azusa Street to other parts of the city. Others tried to assume the role, like

William Durham and Florence Crawford, but no one person emerged as a leader who could consolidate the work.

A closer look at the events that took place at Azusa unveils three key reasons for the eventual disintegration of the work: (1) racism, (2) doctrinal controversy, and (3) personal strife.

RACISM

In the beginning, the meetings were integrated and glorious. Despite the fact that Seymour was black, many of his followers were white. While at the beginning of the revival, blacks did predominate, it was at the height of the meetings that whites constituted a majority.

The staff of the Azusa Street Mission (later incorporated as Apostolic Faith Mission) was an integrated staff of men and women, blacks and whites. Frank Bartleman, in reporting on the Azusa revival, praised the work and stated that the color line had been washed away in the Blood. The passionate desire for sanctification as well as a great hunger for God brought people together of varying races during a time of racial oppression and segregation upheld by the Jim Crow laws of those days.

In April 1907, a full year after the beginning of the Azusa Street revival, *The Apostolic Faith* continued to make the same point: "The Church is composed of people from all races and nations who, by the blood of Christ, have been made into a family." But this time of worshiping together in racial harmony was coming to an end.

In addition to the derogatory remarks made by Parham concerning the emotionalism, he also made racist remarks. When Parham visited Azusa Street at Seymour's invitation in October 1906, he denounced the revival as a "darky camp meeting."[2]

Another pressure that was placed on those precious meetings at Azusa was the barrage of racist remarks in the local Los Angeles newspapers. One reporter labeled such events as "disgusting scenes." "Whites and Blacks Mix in a Religious Frenzy," he announced. Another paper thundered, "Religious Fanaticism Creates Wild Scenes," "Holy Kickers Carry On Mad Orgies," and "Negroes and Whites Give Themselves Over to Strange Outbursts of Zeal." Such headlines were designed to inflame the imagination, titillating the casual reader with sexual innuendo like a supermarket tabloid."[3]

Caricatures in the Los Angeles Times newspaper
(Used by permission, Flower Pentecostal Heritage Center)

Before long, whites were leaving the work at Azusa Street and going to other churches. Bartleman reports in his book that in September 1906, "A brother, Elmer Fisher, then started another mission at 327 South Spring Street, known as the Upper Room Mission. Most of the white saints from Azusa went with him, with the baptized ones from the New Testament Church."[4]

Florence Crawford and Clara Lum, who helped Seymour publish *The Apostolic Faith*, moved to Portland and started an almost exclusive work for whites.

Once the whites defected, the Azusa Street Mission became almost entirely black. As a result, Seymour revised the doctrines, discipline, and constitution of his Apostolic Faith movement to recognize himself as "bishop" and guarantee that the successor would always be "a man of color."

Seymour struggled with the painful consequences as he watched the disintegration of the work over racial prejudice. Finally, in May 1914, the Apostolic Mission held a business meeting to amend its articles of incorporation and to elect new trustees. "The new constitution required that the bishop, vice-bishop, and all trustees were to be 'people of color.'"[5]

In 1915, Seymour wrote a 95-page book, *The Doctrines and Disciplines of the Azusa Street Apostolic Faith Mission of Los Angeles.* In the book, we get a glimpse of his heart on the matter of racial conflict.

> Our colored brethren must love our white brethren and respect them in truth so that the Word of God can have free course, and our white brethren must love their colored brethren and respect them in the truth so that the Holy Spirit won't be grieved. I hope we won't have any more trouble and division spirit.[6]

DOCTRINAL CONTROVERSIES

In the history of revival, as men's hearts have been warmed by the fires of the Holy Spirit, doctrinal controversy has always been close behind. What men have experienced in their hearts has been succeeded by what men have encountered in their heads. The revival at Azusa Street was no different. As racism created breaks in the original unity and joy at Azusa, doctrinal disagreements also emerged to break the unity. These controversies centered on the doctrine of sanctification and the doctrine of the trinity.

SANCTIFICATION

In this book, we have learned that the Pentecostal movement emerged from the Holiness movement of the 1800s. John Wesley taught that through an instantaneous experience, some time after conversion, a believer could become entirely sanctified (a state of Christian perfection). Seizing upon this understanding of sanctification, Pentecostals have called it the "baptism of the Holy Spirit," which is evidenced by the experience of speaking in tongues. Like other Methodists, Parham believed that sanctification was a second work of grace, separate from salvation. But he also adopted the more radical Holiness belief in a third experience—the "baptism with the Holy Spirit and fire." His student, William Seymour, carried this belief in the association of sanctification and the baptism in the Spirit, to Azusa, believing that Spirit baptism was the key to sanctification.

This controversy exploded when William Durham, the Los Angeles preacher, opposed the position and in a conference in Chicago in 1910, challenged their teaching, proposing a gradual process of sanctification in which the sanctifying work of Christ was "appropriated" over one's life. Durham invited Howard Goss, former associate of Parham, to the conference. Goss became convinced that Durham was right and rejected the second work of grace as taught by Parham.

Durham then carried the message of the "Finished Work of Calvary" with him from Chicago, Illinois, to Los Angeles, California, where he was locked out of Azusa because of his teachings on sanctification. When he was not allowed to preach his message in the Azusa Street Mission, Durham rented a building at the corner of Seventh and Los Angeles Streets. From his pulpit, he continued to proclaim his message of the "Finished Work of Calvary." Frank Bartleman, Glenn Cook, and Frank J. Ewart eventually accepted his message and then helped propagate the message across North America.[7]

Charles Parham became incensed by the teachings of Durham. In January 1912, he prayed that God would reveal to the world whose teachings were right by taking the life of the teacher who was in error—that summer, Durham died of tuberculosis. This is not to say that God got involved in this controversy among men, but Parham believed that God had answered his prayer.[8]

The "Finished Work of Calvary" message divided the Pentecostal movement and was accepted at the formation of the Assemblies of God in 1914 and later by most Oneness Pentecostal organizations, including the United Pentecostal Church International. It is interesting to note that most white Pentecostals accepted the "finished work" doctrine, and most black Pentecostals held to the "second work" truth as originally preached by Seymour.

THE TRINITY

The next hot issue that emerged in the early 1900s was the conflict over the Trinity. In the decade following Azusa Street, a number of Pentecostals began to question the proper formula for baptism. While most evangelicals believe in baptizing in the name of the Father, Son, and the Holy Spirit, a group emerged that believed in baptizing in "Jesus' name." It was revealed to Charles Parham that people should be baptized in Jesus' name, into the name of the Father, Son, and Holy Ghost. Others began to adopt this doctrinal position as well. While Jesus had commanded baptism in the name of the Father, the Son, and the Holy Spirit, these individuals noted that the baptisms in the Book of Acts were in the name of Jesus only. With this understanding, some began to baptize and rebaptize in Jesus' name only.

During the early Pentecostal movement, Woodworth-Etter was in continual demand, becoming a featured speaker at the Worldwide Pentecostal Camp Meeting at Arroyo Seco, California. In April 1913, while she was holding a camp meeting there, R.A. McAllister, a Canadian who had been baptized in the Spirit at Azusa, was asked to teach.

McAllister discussed the baptismal formula indicating that the disciples were baptized in Jesus' name. That evening, John G. Scheppe, who was attending the meetings, was overwhelmed by this new thought. "The following morning, Scheppe ran through the camp shouting that God had given him a revelation that believers were to be baptized in the name of 'Jesus only.'"[9]

But what began as a baptismal formula soon led to a denial of the Trinity. By the spring of 1914, Frank Ewart, a former associate of Durham, accepted the "new found truth" and became one of its leading advocates. Ewart reached the conclusion that the singular "name" in Matthew 28:19 was Jesus Christ. He came to believe that the one true God who had revealed Himself as Father, in the Son, and as the Holy Spirit was none other than Jesus Christ.

Ewart explained his discovery to other Pentecostal ministers, some of whom rejected his teaching, but others enthusiastically embraced it. On April 15, 1914, Ewart rebaptized Glenn A. Cook, his assistant and a veteran evangelist of the Azusa Street Mission, in the name of Jesus Christ, and Cook rebaptized Ewart. This would set in motion an issue that would divide the Pentecostal movement between the Trinitarians and the Jesus Name only, or Oneness, believers. After Ewart and Cook were rebaptized, they rebaptized thousands of Pentecostals with the shorter newfound formula "in Jesus' name."

Among those who accepted the Oneness doctrine in the early period was Elder Garfield Thomas Haywood, an African-American minister from Indianapolis, who pastored a very successful Pentecostal church, Christ Temple of the Apostolic Faith Assembly, which had in 1913, between 400-500 members. Christ Temple was one of the largest Pentecostal churches and congregations in the world. The racial make-up of the congregation was about 50 percent African-American and 50 percent white.

Bishop Haywood was rebaptized in the name of Jesus. Subsequently, he rebaptized his entire congregation in the name of Jesus.

The issue would continue to divide the Pentecostals until 1916. In St. Louis, J. Roswell Flower, an opponent of the Jesus Only movement, called a meeting in an effort to squelch the burgeoning group. The Statements of Fundamental Truths that were adopted at the meeting rejected the Oneness theology. The result was that over one quarter of those attending walked out in opposition—including Ewart, Goss, and Haywood. The result caused an already damaged Pentecostal movement, because of race issues and sanctification, to become even more broken over the Oneness theology.

The revival that began with such promise of unity faced its greatest challenge. Ultimately, it failed as hundreds of different Pentecostal groups emerged during the next hundred years. Frank Bartleman's words ring true in the light of the controversies at the beginning of the 20th century.

> Every fresh division or party in the church gives to the world a contradiction as to the oneness of the body of Christ, and the truthfulness of the Gospel. Multitudes are bowing down and burning incense to a doctrine rather than Christ. ...The Spirit is laboring for the unity of believers today, for the "one body," that the prayer of Jesus may be answered, "that they all may be one, that the world may believe"[10]

Endnotes

1. Goff, *Fields White Unto Harvest*, 132.

2. William C. Turner, Jr., "Movements in the Spirit: A Review of African American Holiness/Pentecostal/Apostolics," in Wardell Payne, ed., *Directory of African American Religious Bodies* (Washington, D.C.: Howard University Press, 1991), 251.

3. http://www.pctii.org/pccna/papers/west.html

4. Bartleman, *Azusa Street*, 9.

5. Martin, *The Life and Ministry of William Seymour*, 325.

6. Ibid., 327.

7. Anderson, *Visions of the Disinherited*, 106.

8. Martin, *The Life and Ministry of William Seymour*, 289.

9. Martin, *The Life and Ministry of William Seymour*, 290.

10. Bartleman, *Azusa Street*.

Chapter Ten

BEYOND THE WAVE OF REVIVAL

SEYMOUR, though having problems with his heart, continued to attend the meetings. And in spite of all the controversies and divisions, the spirit of Azusa spread around the world. The first wave of "Azusa pilgrims" journeyed throughout the United States, spreading the Pentecostal fire, primarily in Holiness churches, missions, and camp meetings. And eventually, so many missionaries spread the word from Azusa that within two years the movement had spread to over 50 nations.

Stories of the revival spread quickly across North America to Europe and other parts of the world as participants traveled, testified, and published articles in sympathetic Holiness publications. As mentioned previously, of particular influence was *The Apostolic Faith* newspaper issued occasionally between September 1906 and May 1908 through the labors of William Seymour and Clara Lum, editors. Distributed without charge, thousands of ministers and laypersons received copies at home and overseas. Five thousand copies of the first edition (September 1906) were printed, and by 1907 the press run reached 50,000.

American Pentecostal pioneers who received tongues at Azusa Street went back to their homes to spread the movement among their own people, at times against great opposition. One of the first was Gaston Barnabas Cashwell of North Carolina, who spoke in tongues in 1906. His six-month preaching tour of the South in 1907 resulted in major inroads among Southern Holiness folk. Under his ministry, Cashwell saw several Holiness denominations swept into the new movement, including the Church of God (Cleveland, Tennessee), the Pentecostal Holiness Church, the Fire-Baptized Holiness Church, and the Pentecostal Free-Will Baptist Church.

Pentecostalism grew from occurrences of speaking in tongues in the southern Appalachians (1896), Topeka, Kansas (1901), and Los Angeles (1906). Working independently, Holiness movement preachers, W.R. Spurling and A. J. Tomlinson in the South, Charles Fox Parham in Topeka, and William Seymour in Los Angeles, each convinced of general apostasy in American Christianity, preached and prayed for religious revival. The largest Pentecostal body in the United States is presently the Assemblies of God, with an inclusive membership of over 2.1 million. Today the Pentecostal movement is recognized the world over and is particularly strong in South America.

AIMEE SEMPLE MCPHERSON[1]

Born Aimee Elizabeth Kennedy in Salford, Ontario, Canada, she was the daughter of James Morgan Kennedy, a widower and devout Methodist, and Mildred Ona Pearce, 36 years his junior, who had been hired to nurse his wife during her terminal illness.

Aimee was raised in an atmosphere of strong Christian beliefs. As a teenager, however, she became an avowed atheist, and began her public speaking career at the age of 13 in this context, writing letters to the newspaper defending evolution, debating local clergy, and addressing other issues. She met her first husband, Robert James Semple, a Pentecostal missionary from Ireland, in December 1907, while attending a revival meeting at the urging of her father. After her conversion and a short courtship, they were married on August 12, 1908. Shortly thereafter, the two embarked on an evangelical tour, first to Europe and then to China, where they arrived in June 1910. Shortly after they disembarked in Hong Kong, however, they both contracted malaria, and Robert Semple died of the disease on August 19, 1910. Aimee recovered and gave birth to a daughter, Roberta Star Semple, on September 17, after which she returned to the United States.

Sister Amiee

While in New York, she met her second husband, Harold Stewart McPherson, an accountant. They were married on May 5, 1912, and they had a son, Rolf Potter Kennedy McPherson, born March 23, 1913.

In 1916, she toured through the Southern United States in her "Gospel Car," a 1912 Packard touring car with religious slogans painted on the side. Standing in the back seat of the convertible, she would give sermons through a bullhorn. On the road between sermons, she would sit in the backseat typing sermons and other religious materials. By 1917, she had started her own newspaper entitled, *The Bridal Call*, for which she wrote many of the articles.

From 1918 to 1922, McPherson was an itinerant Pentecostal preacher, finally settling with her mother in Los Angeles, California, and founding the Foursquare Gospel church. She supervised construction of a large, domed church building in the Echo Park area of Los Angeles, and it was completed in June 1923. Named Angelus Temple, it had a seating capacity of over 5,000.

At the time, women in the pulpit ministry were rare; those who wore makeup and jewelry in the pulpit, nonexistent. However, McPherson's uniqueness in this respect, her flamboyance and her unashamed use of low-key sex appeal to attract converts, endeared her to crowds of followers in Los Angeles. She would invariably appear before parishioners in a white gown, carrying a bouquet of flowers.

Unlike her contemporary, Billy Sunday, McPherson was less a fire-and-brimstone preacher and more prone to endorse charitable work and "ecstatic" facets of worship. These traits also increased her popularity.

McPherson began broadcasting on radio in its infancy of the early '20s. She was the first woman in history to preach a radio sermon, and with the opening of Foursquare Gospel-owned KFSG on February 6, 1924, she also became the first woman to be granted a broadcast license by the Federal Communications Commission.

McPherson was also very skillful at fundraising. Collections were taken at every meeting, usually with the admonishment of "no coins, please." When the $1.5 million Angelus Temple opened its doors, construction was already entirely paid for through private donations.

McPherson was not universally loved, though. For example, a group of Ku Klux Klan members once attended one of her meetings expecting a blessing, and were instead rebuked by McPherson for their racism. She also gained the animosity of several government officials and organized crime figures, as a result of "naming names," which often occurred on her radio shows.

During the Great Depression, McPherson was active in creating soup kitchens, free clinics, and other charitable activities. With the outbreak of World War II, she also became involved in war bond rallies.

On September 27, 1944, she was found dead of an overdose of prescription barbiturates. Once again, rumors flew, this time conjecturing suicide. It is generally agreed, though, that the overdose was accidental, as is stated on the coroner's report.

McPherson is buried in Forest Lawn Memorial Park Cemetery in Glendale, California. According to *The Preachers* by James Morris, she was buried with a live telephone in her casket to ensure her survival in the event of bodily resurrection, although other biographers do not mention this and groundskeepers at Forest Lawn deny it. The Foursquare Gospel church, whose leadership was assumed by McPherson's son, Rolf, for 44 years after her death, continues worldwide with over two million members, over 90 percent of whom live outside the United States.[2]

LATTER RAIN MOVEMENT

The Latter Rain movement began in 1948 in North Battleford, Saskatchewan, Canada, led by George Hawtin and P.G. Hunt. In 1947, they had attended a meeting held by William Branham and were so impressed with the supernatural manifestations that they were encouraged to seek God for the same types of manifestation of the gifts of the Holy Spirit in their lives. These brethren had an organization and location called "Sharon," also known as the Sharon Brethren, and they published a newsletter titled, *The Sharon Star*.

Hawtin pioneered a Bible institute as a Pentecostal Assemblies of Canada pastor in 1935. He later resigned in 1947 and joined Herrick Holt's "Sharon's Global Missions" as president. Shortly after, a revival in the Bible school afforded him a leading role in the resulting movement. His leadership was rapidly eclipsed, though, as others assumed leadership roles. Myrtle Beall, another key figure in the Latter Rain movement, founded the Bethesda Missionary Temple with a 3,000-seat building—all from a Sunday school ministry. Originally an Assembly of God church, the Bethesda Temple withdrew its membership, as it became a center of the Latter Rain movement. It provided direction for many North

American churches. Beall's son, James, succeeded her as senior pastor in the late 1970s and was an influential Charismatic renewal leader and contributed to many Charismatic journals. Myrtle's daughter, Patricia Gruits, authored an important book, *Understanding God* (1962), which has influenced many churches' theology in the United States.

The Latter Rain movement was characterized by many healings and miraculous phenomena and included an emphasis on spiritual gifts that were received by the laying on of hands.

The doctrinal system of the Latter Rain included Pentecostalism's baptism of the Spirit with the evidence of speaking in tongues and the New Pentecostal deliverance revivals' miraculous healing thrust. But the fiery movement had its own distinctiveness as well. There were primarily six new teachings that shaped the Latter Rain movement:

Restorationism. The further development of restoration theology views God as progressively restoring truths to the church since the Reformation.

Fivefold Ministry. The teaching that God is restoring apostles and prophets to the church to function with the three other gifted offices: evangelists, pastors, and teachers (see Eph. 4:11). Apostles and prophets provide direction with new revelations that play a major role in paving the way for Christ's second coming.

Laying on of the Hands. A ritual performed by modern apostles and prophets to impart the Holy Spirit and other spiritual blessings and gifts.

Prophecy. The practice of "personal prophecy" is being restored to the church. Prophecy is no longer restricted to general words of exhortation but includes personal detailed revelations for guidance and instruction.

Recovery of True Worship. The belief that God's manifested presence is dependent upon a certain order of worship involving singing in tongues, clapping, shouting, singing prophecies, and a new order of praise dancing.

Unity of the Faith. The doctrine that the church, usually perceived to be a band of overcomers in neo-Pentecostal ranks, will attain unity in the faith before Christ returns.

THE HEALING EVANGELISTS

John Alexander Dowie and Charles Parham were among the first to really preach the gospel of healing. Through their teaching and practice, hundreds were healed. Their influence would send forth a company of men and women who were powerfully gifted evangelists, and they would extend the fires of Pentecost to a new generation. As mentioned previously, some of these earlier healing evangelists actually had relationships with John Dowie and the work at Zion.

JOHN G. LAKE

John G. Lake, a businessman influenced by the healing ministry of John Alexander Dowie, was born in 1870 and died in 1935. He received the baptism of the Holy Spirit in 1907 in the wake of the Azusa Street revival and became known for his ministry as a missionary and "faith healer." His life and message are represented in a book compiled by Roberts Liardon, titled, *John G. Lake: The Complete Collection of His Life Teachings.* The following biographical details were gathered from that book.

Lake was originally from Ontario, Canada and grew up in a large family who continually suffered with illness. His childhood memories were filled with seeing someone in the house either sick, dying, or dead. Lake eventually became an industrious businessman and started two newspapers before beginning a very successful career in real estate. By the time he left for the mission field, he walked away from a yearly salary of $50,000 (around 1 million in 2005 dollars), as well as his seat on the Chicago Board of Trade.

Early in his career, Lake's dearly loved wife fell ill with a life-threatening illness. Having a lifetime of suffering and bereavement behind him, he refused to accept her illness, and took the radical step of taking her to see John Alexander Dowie. Through Dowie's prayer of faith, Lake's wife was healed, and Lake was drawn into Dowie's movement. He eventually became an elder in the church, and it was here that he captured his passion for divine healing, with increasing success.

Lake's greatest ministry was in South Africa, and his ministry there had dramatic and far-reaching consequences. Lake's arrival began a major revival that started both the largest white and black Pentecostal denominations in that country to date.

Lake's ministry was unique, and he established relationships with many of the leading figures of his day, including Cecil Rhodes, Mahatma Ghandi, Conan Doyle, and railroad tycoon, James J. Hill, and others. Rhodes reported that "Lake's message swept Africa. He has done more toward South Africa's future peace than any other man." Ghandi was reported to have said that "Dr. Lake's teachings will eventually be accepted by the entire world." He had an almost unparalleled vision of Christianity and its potential.

Perhaps the most outstanding feature of his ministry was the repeatability of the miracles he witnessed. After his ministry in South Africa, he returned to the United States and settled in Spokane, Washington, where he established healing rooms, and saw tens of thousands healed either under his hands or those he trained. The city was even declared at one point to be the "healthiest city in America." When he was challenged that he could not repeat the same miracles in another city, he moved to Portland and saw similar results.

Although he founded a number of institutions, they never gained the widespread prominence of other similar ministries. His daughter, Gertrude, and her husband, Wilfred Reidt, carried on his ministry until late in their lives when they officially passed the ministry to a young minister named Curry Blake. Blake had been run over by a car as a baby, but while in the hospital, his mother prayed for him and he miraculously recovered with barely any sign of what was thought to be a life-threatening injury. Unknown to the Blake family at the time, this event occurred exactly 20 years after Lake had given a prophecy about a successor who would come 20 years later. Blake has begun to rebuild Lake's ministries and vision. Many claim Lake as a spiritual influence, but Blake's success in the healing ministry, as well as the extent of his vision of Christianity is uniquely reminiscent of Lake himself.

F.F. BOSWORTH

Little is known of the early life of F.F. Bosworth. His family moved to John Dowie's Zion city when he was young, and both he and his brother "BB" became preachers.

Bosworth strongly influenced many of the early healing evangelists, including Oral Roberts, T.L. Osborne, John G. Lake, and many others. In 1924, he published his classic book on healing, *Christ the Healer*, dealing with the principles of healing through the finished work of Christ on the cross at Calvary. It is still in print today having had 31 editions published by 1997 and over 150,000 copies printed.

Bosworth worked with John Alexander Dowie for a number of years before starting his own healing ministry. Bosworth embraced Pentecostalism as a result of being influenced by Charles Parham in 1906 and was also influenced by E.W. Kenyon and his teachings on Divine healing.

Bosworth's reputation spread rapidly throughout the 1920s as a result of a number of healing campaigns that he held throughout North America and Canada. He also established "The National Radio Revival Missionary Crusaders" and began broadcasting in Chicago with a tremendous response from the listeners. He eventually met another renowned healing evangelist, William Branham and supported Branham from 1948 until he died in 1958.

WILLIAM BRANHAM

William Branham, born in 1909 and died in 1965, was considered one of the greatest of the Pentecostal healers. Branham was a Baptist

preacher in Indiana, but in 1946 everything changed. Branham reported that an angel instructed him to carry the gift of healing to the
world, and from that point forward, Branham began a successful evangelistic and healing ministry.

William Branham

Respecting this powerful ministry, Pastor Jack Moore, a Oneness
preacher in Louisiana, connected Branham with Gordon Lindsay who
was well-known and respected in the Pentecostal circles.
Consequently, Lindsay agreed to become his road manager. Ern Baxter,
a former Pentecostal preacher from Vancouver, also joined the team
and taught at Branham's meetings.

Branham was respected for his ministry in the word of knowledge.
He would often reveal intimate details about a person's life while ministering to them.[3] And through a gift of healing, he was also able to
detect people's physical problems through a "vibrating" in his left
hand.

THE VOICE OF HEALING

James Gordon Lindsay was born in Zion City, Illinois, in 1906 to parents who were disciples of John Alexander Dowie, the father of healing revivalism in America. After the family moved to Portland, Oregon, the young boy was influenced by John G. Lake and converted by Charles G. Parham. At the age of 18, he began his ministry as a traveling evangelist conducting meetings in Assembly of God churches and other Pentecostal groups.

When World War II broke out, Lindsay accepted a call to become pastor of a church in Ashland, Oregon. Then in 1947, he resigned his position as pastor to become William Branham's manager. Soon after, Lindsay's publication, *The Voice of Healing*, appeared in 1948. Then, Branham announced his retirement from the revival circuit. The news came as quite a blow to Lindsay who along with Jack and Anna Jeanne Moore had just begun the revival publication to cover Branham's meetings. The publication continued, covering revivals and other evangelists, and it was circulated nationwide.

The group sponsored the first convention of healing evangelists in Dallas, Texas, during December 1949. *The Voice of Healing* began to function as a loose fellowship of ministers. As the popularity of some members rose, they left the fellowship to establish their own organizations and publish their own literature.

Lindsay's own work moved in the direction of missions. He sponsored missions programs in several foreign countries and started a radio ministry. During 1956, he conducted a Winning the Nations Crusade, sending teams of ministers all around the world. *The Voice of Healing* magazine changed names briefly to *World-Wide Revival* in 1968 before the final change to *Christ for the Nations*.

Lindsay was a very productive writer, publishing over 250 volumes of historical and doctrinal books on the healing revival movement. His ministry came to a halt, however, with his sudden death on April 1, 1973. Lindsay's wife, Freda, and daughter, Carole, continued the work he began. Christ for the Nations, Inc. has five main facets: a national church program; a national literature work; a Jewish mission in Israel; a Bible training school in Dallas; and a prayer and tape ministry. Christ for the Nations continues to be a successful ministry having trained thousands of young people for the ministry.

ORAL ROBERTS

Oral Roberts was born on January 24, 1918 in Pontotoc County, Oklahoma as Granville "Oral" Roberts, the fifth and youngest child of Rev. and Mrs. Ellis M. Roberts. His mother was one-quarter Cherokee.

After graduating from high school, his higher education consisted of about two years of college study at Bible schools in Oklahoma on a part-time basis. In 1938, he married a preacher's daughter, Evelyn Lutman Fahnestock. Their marriage lasted 66 years until her death on May 4, 2005. During their life together, they expanded his ministry from preaching in tents to preaching on the radio. Roberts eventually made his way to television and attracted a huge audience. He has written more than 120 books such as *Miracle of Seed-Faith* and his autobiography, *Expect a Miracle*.

In 1947, Oral Roberts resigned his pastoral ministry to found Oral Roberts Evangelistic Association. He has conducted more than 300 evangelistic and healing crusades on six continents and has appeared as a guest speaker for hundreds of national and international meetings and conventions. He later founded Oral Roberts University in Tulsa, Oklahoma in 1963, stating he was obeying a command from God. The university was chartered in 1963 and received the first students in 1965. Another part of the Oral Roberts Evangelistic Association is the Abundant Life Prayer Group, which operates day and night. Mostly made up of students, the group receives thousands of calls for prayer daily from around the world.

In 1980, Oral Roberts said he had a vision of a 900-foot-tall Jesus who encouraged him to continue the construction of his City of Faith

Medical and Research Center, which opened in 1981. It included three skyscrapers, the tallest being Cityplex Tower which stands 648 feet tall with 60 floors. It is the second tallest building in Oklahoma. At the time, it was the largest health facility of its kind in the world and sought to merge prayer and medicine in the healing process.

The City of Faith was in operation for only eight years before closing in late 1989. The Orthopedic Hospital of Oklahoma still operates on these premises. The Cityplex Tower is currently utilized as office space and Cityplex West Tower (30 floors and 106,348 feet) is still used as a hospital.

As of this book's printing, Oral Roberts lives in Southern California and continues to minister on a limited basis.

KATHRYN KUHLMAN

In a world ravaged by disease and spiritual darkness, Kathryn Kuhlman offered people hope. Through her miracle services, held from the early 1950s until her death in 1976, thousands of people were healed and countless others committed their lives to Christ.

Kathryn was born on May 9, 1907, on a farm outside Concordia, Missouri, and was saved at a revival meeting when she was 14 years old. Two years later, she left home to travel with her sister and brother-in-law, Myrtle and Everett Parrott, who held tent revivals in the Northwest and Midwest. She stayed with them until she was 21, the year she set out on her own as a preacher.

Although her first sermon was in a small, dirty pool hall in a run-down section of Boise, Idaho, Kathryn built a strong name for herself as she preached in tents and slept in poultry barns in Idaho, Utah, and Colorado.

She settled down in 1933 and opened Colorado's highly successful Denver Revival Tabernacle. People from across the country came to hear Kathryn, and big-name evangelists came to preach in her pulpit. For five years, the ministry blossomed and fostered a great revival in the area. However, her promising ministry was compromised when Evangelist Burroughs Waltrip, Sr. came to preach.

Kathryn Kuhlman

Waltrip divorced his wife and abandoned his two young sons shortly after meeting Kathryn. He then moved to Iowa, started a radio program and church, and kept his past a secret. When he and Kathryn married on October 18, 1938, she gave up her church in Denver and tried preaching at revivals around the Midwest. Her attempts to preach were thwarted, however, when church leaders discovered her past and asked her to leave.

The rejections that Kathryn endured made her realize she could not preach and remain married to a scandalously divorced man. She decided to leave Waltrip in 1944. Kathryn said she died to the flesh that day and put aside the desires of her heart so she could fully serve God.

She finally found a safe haven from gossip and a hungry people to feed with the gospel when she arrived in Franklin, Pennsylvania, in

1946. Kathryn started a popular radio program and a church there and built a ministry that was followed by miracles, signs, and wonders. It was in Franklin that she came to understand the power of the Holy Spirit and the miracle of healing.

In 1948, Kathryn moved to Pittsburgh where she lived for the rest of her life. She held her famous miracle services in Carnegie Hall for 20 years, filling the great auditorium to capacity every time. People all over the world clamored to her miracle services and listened intently to her radio and television shows.

Kathryn Kuhlman died on February 20, 1976 from an enlarged heart, yet her passing did not end her ministry. She left behind a legacy of instruction on miracles, healing, and the power of the Holy Spirit.[4]

A. A. ALLEN

In the history of the healing revival of the 1950s and 1960s, another healing evangelist arrived on the scene, Rev. A.A. Allen. Gifted, dramatic, and controversial, A.A. Allen was a self-made success, largely through his unerring faith in God's sovereign power and boundless compassion. Remarkable healings of all kinds occurred in his giant citywide crusades, and he became renowned for his ability to exorcise demonic spirits from the most difficult cases through his powerful prayers and daring faith. No sickness or crippling disease was too tough for Allen to tackle.

Rev. Allen burst onto the scene as a dynamic, flamboyant tent evangelist. He was an eloquent preacher who was genuinely concerned about the rights of minorities and the financially deprived. The warm relationship that Allen developed with his predominately poor and ethnically diverse audiences undoubtedly stemmed from his own abused and impoverished adolescent years. He was one of the first citywide revivalists to defy and break the segregation barrier in the deep South by fully integrating his audiences.

Another factor in A.A. Allen's success was the message of hope that he preached to the poor and underprivileged. They flocked to his meetings to sing and shout their way to victory and deliverance. Allen made all of them feel important to God's work and Kingdom. For the crowds of the poor and deprived, Allen's message was a welcome challenge. They could hope and believe that a better quality of life was not just attainable, but was actually God's promise to every believer.

In 1958, he built a Christian community in Miracle Valley, Arizona, that became a permanent headquarters, including a Bible training center to prepare young men and women for ministry as pastors, evangelists, teachers, and musicians. Miracle Valley became a "spiritual mecca" for believers from around the world, with thousands attending the Camp Meetings and Conventions conducted by Rev. Allen and his staff. Miracle Valley was an energetic facility for radio and television production, and housed one of America's largest independent church printing and distribution centers for magazines, books, recordings, and a variety of Christian literature. Allen's ministry would eventually reach out to the poor and suffering in other nations as well through evangelistic crusades, Bible schools, and feeding programs in disadvantaged areas.

In 1970, A.A. Allen died unexpectedly with some controversy over the nature of his death.

T.L. AND DAISY OSBORNE

T.L. Osborne and his wife, Daisy, began in Oklahoma as evangelists, and in1945, they went to India as missionaries but returned because of ill health and disappointment over the lack of success on the mission field. Later, while pastoring a church in Portland, Oregon, they began to seek God for the answers to world evangelism. The answer was "signs and wonders," and they left the church to enter into evangelistic work. Their work over the years has been very successful, due, to a large part, to the signs and wonders that were demonstrated in their meetings. In 1948, they found their way to Jamaica, where there were scores of healings and hundreds of conversions. After returning to the United States for some highly successful campaigns with other major healing evangelists, they went to Puerto Rico in 1951, where there were over 18,000 conversions within 12 days. Then they went to Cuba where thousands more came to Christ. From that point on, the fruitfulness of their ministry continued to increase.

They traveled to over 76 nations of the world, and their crusades became the pattern for mass evangelism.[5]

The Charismatic Movement

The next great expansion of the Pentecostal movement would happen in the 1960s and is called the Charismatic movement—when Pentecostalism spread into the mainline denominations. The defining point for this movement probably happened ten years before the movement gained notoriety when, in 1951, the Full Gospel Business Men's Fellowship International (FGBMFI) was formed. The president of FGBMFI was Demos Shakarian who was the catalyst for integrating the Pentecostal experience into both mainline Protestant as well as Catholic churches. He and Oral Roberts brought together mainline clergy and laity to interact in a nonthreatening setting with blue-collar Pentecostals. It has been said that in the early years, the Pentecostal movement found its greatest audience among the less refined of society. Of course, this was not totally true, but it was a stereotype attached to Pentecostals. This misconception changed with the integration of the two groups and the introduction of the Pentecostal experience to Protestant denominations. The FGBMFI conferences brought thousands of people together, and they were introduced to dynamic worship and testimonies from businessmen and women who had been baptized in the Spirit. FGBMFI chapters began to sprout up in almost every city in America, paving the way for the coming renewal.

Two events signal the historical beginning of the Charismatic movement, one in the West and one in the East. When Dennis Bennett, rector of St. Mark's Episcopal Church in Van Nuys, California, was baptized in the Spirit, the Charismatic movement got its launch on the West Coast. Under the influence of a local group of Charismatic laypeople, Bennett led 100 others toward receiving baptism and speaking in tongues. Though he was forced to resign his parish, his case brought national attention creating an emergence to the limelight of other Protestant Charismatics who had pre-dated him in their experience. His book, *Nine O'clock in the Morning*, told the dramatic story of how he was baptized in the Spirit and spoke in tongues. Logos Publishers, founded by Dan Malachuk, was the publishing company that for the next 15 to 20 years was the source of a new collection of testimonial and teaching books for the Charismatic and Pentecostal movement.

In 1967 at Duquesne University in Pittsburgh, the Holy Spirit was poured out on a Catholic prayer group observing a midnight vigil. While in some circles Catholics were hardly thought to be Christians, much less candidates for the Pentecostal experience, this event launched the Catholic Charismatic movement, and thousands of Catholics were baptized in the Spirit, including priests and nuns.

John and Elizabeth Sherrill played a key role in those days through the books they wrote, the first book being a classic introduction to the Charismatic movement, *They Speak with Other Tongues*, tracing John Sherrill's investigation into the phenomenon of speaking in tongues. He relates the historical and biblical background, examines significant contemporary events, shares his personal experience, and provides valuable insight into the gift of the Holy Spirit.

Members of the Episcopalian Church, John Sherrill and his wife are coauthors of numerous best-sellers, including *The Hiding Place*, *The Cross and the Switchblade*, and *God's Smuggler*. The Sherrills served on the staff of *Guideposts* Magazine for 20 years and were founding publishers of Chosen Books, a division of Fleming Revell.

From the West coast to the East coast, the Spirit was baptizing people in many church denominations—Catholics, Episcopals, and Methodists—then keeping them there to help the Spirit bring revival to those denominations. Hundreds of little prayer groups sprang up all over the country where these new Pentecostals could worship and minister to one another in the gifts of the Spirit.

CHARISMATICS, PENTECOSTALS, AND THE MEDIA

As mentioned previously, Aimee Semple McPherson was the first Pentecostal to use media to reach the masses. Then in the '50s, Oral Roberts made the transition from radio to television, and thousands of people regularly viewed his weekly program.

Since those early days, the Pentecostals and the Charismatics have dominated the Christian television marketing, including "The 700 Club" and Trinity Broadcasting Network. Smaller networks like Daystar and Inspiration are also Pentecostal/Charismatic in their programming.

In the publishing world, they have also made their mark. *The Herald of Faith* served as a fellowship magazine for the Independent Assemblies of God until about 1958. When Mattsson-Boze left the Philadelphia Church in 1958, he took with him the *Herald of Faith* magazine and continued to publish the magazine until 1971, at which time he turned the journal over to Dan Malachuk of Logos International. Logos was particularly identified with the Charismatic "wing" of the movement. Logos' flagship publication was the glossy monthly magazine *Logos Journal*. Malachuk also had a thriving book publishing division, and all publications were sold through religious bookstores, churches, and evangelical ministries.

Jamie Buckingham, through the magazine *Logos Journal*, introduced many Charismatic leaders to a wider audience—leaders such as Dennis Bennett, Bob Mumford, Harold Hill, Merlin Carothers, Iverna Tompkins, and Judson Cornwall, to name a few. Jamie Buckingham edited the *Logos Journal* for a time and wrote 14 books for the company, including the best-seller *Shout it From the Housetops* (1972), written with CBN founder Pat Robertson, and *Daughter of Destiny* (1976), the story of Kathryn Kuhlman.

Eventually, Logos, which had become a household word for many Charismatics, failed in the late '70s, and *Logos Journal* was sold to new owners who renamed it *Charisma*, which is still being published today. Buckingham also worked with Steven Strang of *Charisma* and *Christian Life* Magazines, from 1979 until 1992.

Strang also launched a publishing company, originally called Creation House. Under their label, they have published hundreds of articles about Pentecostals and Charismatics.

In 1983, Don Nori founded a little fledgling Charismatic publishing company called Destiny Image Publishers. Nori, who was working with a local newspaper at the time, went through a period of three days when he had vision after vision concerning the launch of the company. In one of those visions he heard these words, "We publish the prophets." That became the theme for the company as they have published many of the prophetic ministries of the '80s and '90s.

Over the last 23 years, Destiny Image has become one of the largest Charismatic publishing companies in the world. They are best known for publishing Bishop T.D. Jakes' best-selling book (2 million sold), *Woman Thou Art Loosed* and Tommy Tenney's best-seller (1.6 million sold), *The God Chasers*.

Buddy Harrison, along with his wife, Pat, were cofounders of Faith Christian Fellowship International Church, a ministry to pastors. He served as president of the organization from 1978 until he went home to be with the Lord on November 28, 1998.

Harrison was a brother-in-law to Kenneth Hagin and had a prevailing influence within the Word of Faith element of Charismatic circles for more than two decades. In the 1970s, he founded Harrison House, which became a leading publisher of Word-Faith literature. Authors for Harrison House included Kenneth Hagin, Sr., Kenneth and Gloria Copeland, Charles Capps, Joyce Meyer, Roberts Liardon, Oral Roberts, and many others.

In the '90s and turning into the 21st century there have been other revivals and movements that emerged. The Toronto revival and the Brownsville revival attracted hundreds of thousands throughout the 1990s. People came from around the world to experience the power of God demonstrated in their nightly meetings.

Over the last 100 years, since the first days of the Azusa revival, there has been an unprecedented expansion of the Pentecostal message. The Pentecostals and Charismatics have gained a huge foothold within the Christianity community. They are no longer the poor and uneducated—they are found in every walk of life from politics to corporate CEOs.

The Pentecostal experience that exploded at 312 Azusa Street created a paradigm shift that infused new energy and passion into a lifeless, liturgical Christianity. Pentecostals owe a great deal to those pioneers who have gone before. To them we dedicate our renewed energy to continue what they started.

ENDNOTES

1. Liardon, *God's Generals*.

2. Ibid.

3. Eddie Hyatt, *2000 Years of Charismatic History* (Tulsa, OK: Hyatt International Ministries, 1996), 181-182.

4. Liardon, *God's Generals*.

5. Hyatt, *2000 Years of Charismatic History*, 184.

Chapter Eleven

SPEAKING IN TONGUES— GOD'S GIFT TO YOU

The Benefits of Praying In Tongues[1]

IF you've been to any of my meetings, you know that I'm a strong advocate of the development of people's prayer lives; especially in the area of praying in tongues. I emphasize tongues and strong prayer during my messages often because I know how beneficial these things are to a Christian's life. Here are just a few of the benefits of praying in tongues.

Tongues is a Sign

The first benefit of speaking in tongues is that it gives you the assurance that you've been baptized in the Holy Spirit. In my meetings, I often urge those in the congregation to ask the folks next to them if they are saved and filled with the Spirit. Sometimes I will even tell them to ask the person beside them to pray in tongues out loud.

If that person is filled with the Holy Spirit, tongues will flow right out of them. If they're not filled with the Spirit, I will call them forward to receive the baptism. I call that going fishing!

Tongues Will Make You Strong

Another scriptural reason for praying in tongues is that it makes your spirit strong in First Corinthians 14:4 (NKJV) we read:

He who speaks in a tongue edifies himself. . . .

The word "edify" here means to make you spiritually strong. Praying in tongues helps you to become spiritually fit so you can carry out the works of God in the earth. If you have a whimpy spirit, it's possible that you're not praying in tongues enough.

Do you remember that commercial in America a few years ago about Hefty trash bags? It was either "Whimpy, Whimpy, Whimpy," or "Hefty, Hefty, Hefty." You have to decide what kind of container you want to be, a whimpy one, or a Hefty three-ply one. I want to be a Hefty three-ply container so I can hold a lot of God's mighty power!

Tongues Makes You Spiritually Sensitive

Praying in tongues helps you become aware of spiritual events and occurrences. It helps you increase your sensitivity to the workings of the Holy Spirit. People that don't pray in tongues much are not as sharp as they could be in their discerning of the moves of the Holy Spirit and the overall happenings of God.

Tongues Will Build Your Faith

In Jude, verse 20 (NKJV) we find that tongues stirs up our faith. Jude writes:

But you, beloved, building yourselves up on your most holy faith, praying in the Holy Spirit. . . .

Tongues makes your faith come alive! When you get through praying in tongues, you're ready to believe God for anything! It stimulates your ability to trust Him.

Tongues Helps To Clean Up Your Mouth

Praying in the Spirit helps you control the wildest member of your body—your tongue!

Your tongue does more than just taste ice cream, my brother and sister! It brings life or death, blessing or cursing, depending on how you let it be used. (See Proverbs 18:21.) One of the signs of Christian maturity is how much control you have over the conduct of your mouth.

When you pray in tongues a lot, it makes it easier to keep your mouth in subjection to the Holy Spirit. In other words, it helps to break the unruliness of your tongue and clean up your foul talk.

I know that most Christians don't cuss, but bad confessions and unbelief come out of everyone's mouth from time to time. In light of Scripture, unbelief is just as bad as cussing. When you pray in tongues regularly, gossip and accusation will begin to disappear from your speech and holiness will begin to permeate your words and actions.

In James 1:26, it says, *"If any man among you seem to be religious,"* (or spiritual), *"and bridleth not his tongue, but deceiveth his own heart, this man's religion is in vain."*

In James 3:8, we read, *"But the tongue can no man tame; it is unruly evil, full of deadly poison."*

If you are always telling people things you shouldn't be telling them, that means you're not yielding your mouth enough to the Lord. Praying in tongues helps you develop an awareness of the conduct of your mouth.

If there was no other benefit to praying in tongues than just to keep your tongue under control, then that would be reason enough to do it.

Tongues Brings a Spiritual Refreshing

In Isaiah 28 we see that speaking in tongues brings a spiritual refreshing. In verse 11 we read:

For with stammering lips and another tongue will he speak to this people. To whom he said, This is the rest wherewith ye may cause the weary to rest; and

*this is word of the LORD was unto them precept upon precept, precept upon pre-
cept; line upon line, line upon line; here a little, and there a little...*(Isaiah
28:11-13 KJV).

Someone once approached Smith Wigglesworth and said, "Brother
Wigglesworth, don't you ever take a vacation?"

"Every day," he responded. "What do you mean?" "I pray in tongues
daily and I get refreshed. That's my vacation, that's my holiday."

Praying in tongues refreshes you. Have you ever felt like you were
tired, but there was no reason to be tired? When you feel like that, you
need to pray in tongues and cause that refreshing to spring up from
inside of your spirit. Weariness and tiredness will go and strength will
come to you instead.

One way Christians are supposed to find their rest is by praying in
tongues. Praying in tongues helps to keep you fresh, strong, up and
happy. If you pray in tongues every day, you can keep yourself invigor-
ated and refreshed.

Tongues Gives You Power To Be a Witness

Another benefit of tongues is that it gives you power to be a witness.

*"But you shall receive power when the Holy Spirit has come upon you; and you
shall be witnesses to Me in Jerusalem, and in all Judea and Samaria, and to the
end of the earth"* (Acts 1:8 NKJV).

Tongues and The Great Commission

Consider the transformation of the disciples after the Holy Spirit's
outpouring on the day of Pentecost. (See Acts 2.) These men, who formerly had denied Jesus, feared the masses, and fought among themselves about who would be the greatest, were suddenly preaching with
such boldness that the Bible says they turned the world upside down!
(See Acts 17:6.)

After Peter preached on the day of Pentecost, the Bible says three thousand souls were added to the church that very day! (See Acts 2:41.) That's powerful witnessing!

Jesus said tongues would play a major role in the Great Commission. In Mark 16 we read:

And He said to them, *"Go into all the world and preach the gospel to every creature. He who believes and is baptized will be saved; but he who does not believe will be condemned. And these signs will follow those who believe: In My name they will cast out demons; THEY WILL SPEAK WITH NEW TONGUES...* (Mark 16:15-17 NKJV).

A lot of people think that the Great Commission ends with "Go into all the world and preach...," but it continues.

Notice there in verse 17 that it says, *"And they shall speak with new tongues."* More conservative Christians would say that speaking in new tongues means having the knowledge of a foreign language. I can see why they would say that. On the day of Pentecost and during the Azusa Street outpouring of 1906, and even at times today, God gave some the ability to supernaturally speak the natural languages of the earth with fluency. This is one side of the baptism of the Holy Spirit that I think our generation needs to be open to. God will sometimes grant this type of occurrence with the baptism in the Holy Spirit.

Speaking In the Languages of the Earth

I remember hearing these kinds of stories from my grandmother and from others who were a part of early Pentecostalism. When some received the baptism in the Holy Spirit, they began to miraculously speak in a foreign language.

In Topeka, Kansas, in the year of 1901, a minister by the name of Charles Parham began to receive the understanding of what it means to be baptized in the Holy Spirit. A woman by the name of Agnes Ozman was the first to receive the baptism of the Holy Spirit under Parham's ministry. When she received her prayer language, she received the ability to speak a perfect Chinese dialect and write it. This was documented at the time by the United States government. They sent language specialists to Topeka to investigate the outbreak of this phenomena. When the government workers got there, they recorded 20 different languages being spoken, as well as a language they could not interpret.

This happened in the early hours of the Pentecostal movement and I believe that this type of manifestation will begin to happen again in the new millennium.

People also experienced this during the Azusa Street outpouring. Missionaries from Azusa Street were sent to almost every major people group in the world. They believed that whatever earthly language they spoke when they were filled with the Holy Spirit was where they were called to go and preach. If they spoke in an African sounding dialect, they got up, bought a boat ticket and floated over to Africa. When they got off the boat, they spoke their language until somebody understood them and then just went right on preaching.

Some went to China. When they got off the boat and started praying in tongues, their language would activate and the people would start responding! Now that's a call, my brother and sister! That's the way it worked for many of them.

Others were able to speak in a foreign language only periodically and when they got to their mission field, they had to learn the language themselves. Why it worked for some and not others I don't know, but I do believe that when Jesus said, *"And they shall speak with new tongues,"* (Mark 16:17) it included the natural languages of the earth as well as the spiritual languages of the heavens. They work together. This is why the Azusa Street outpouring spread so rapidly throughout the earth. They understood the importance of their prayer language in the role of world evangelism. Speaking in tongues gave them power to be effective witnesses for Christ!

HOW TO MINISTER THE BAPTISM IN THE HOLY SPIRIT

There are at least seven steps to successfully minister the baptism in the Holy Spirit with the evidence of speaking in other tongues. The seven steps are:

Step One

Help the person see that the Holy Spirit has already been poured out. (See Acts 2:4.)

The Holy Spirit was poured out on the day of Pentecost and this powerful gift has been available to believers ever since. Explain to the person that they don't have to beg for the gift of the Holy Spirit, all they have to do is receive it by faith.

Step Two

Show the person receiving that if they are born-again, they are already qualified to receive the gift of the Holy Spirit.

Explain to them that they don't have to somehow clean up their life in order to receive the promise of the Spirit. It's a free gift. All they have to do is ask to receive it. (See Luke11:13.)

Step Three

Tell the person to expect to receive when you lay your hands on them.

The gift of the Holy Spirit is often imparted to believers through the laying on of hands. Before laying hands on them and praying, explain that it is not you who will baptize them with the Holy Spirit, but rather the Lord Jesus Christ. The laying on of hands only serves as a point of contact for them to release their faith.

Step Four

Explain to the person what is about to happen to them and that they are the one who is going to have to open their mouth to do the speaking.

The Holy Spirit will not do the speaking for them! The person receiving will have to open their mouth and yield to the inner flow of the Holy Spirit.

Step Five

Assure them that they will not receive a counterfeit spirit.

In Luke 11:11-13, Jesus said:

If a son asks for bread from any father among you, will he give him a stone? Or if he asks for a fish, will he give him a serpent instead of a fish? Or if he asks for an egg, will he offer him a scorpion? If you then, being evil, know how to give good gifts to your children, how much more will your heavenly Father give the Holy Spirit to those who ask Him! Luke11:11-13 (NKJV)

Step Six

Encourage the person to speak out and act in faith.

Don't allow the person to speak anything in their native language. Tell them to open their mouth by faith and begin to pronounce the various syllables and sounds of their new personal prayer language.

Step Seven

Don't allow a crowd to gather around the person you are ministering to.

Onlookers create confusion and often hinder the person you are praying for from receiving the gift of the Holy Spirit.

HOW TO RECEIVE THE HOLY SPIRIT AND SPEAK WITH TONGUES

And they were all filled with the Holy Spirit and began to speak with other tongues, AS THE SPIRIT GAVE THEM UTTERANCE (Acts 2:4 NKJV).

When seeking the baptism in the Holy Spirit, it's important to recognize that the disciples spoke in tongues *"as the Spirit gave them utterance"* (Acts 2:4). What does that mean? It means that in their spirit they began to hear the voice of the Holy Spirit giving them utterances. They heard the utterances on the inside, but they had to open their mouth and speak them out.

In order to speak in your new prayer language, you have to get your mind quiet so you can hear

what the Holy Spirit is saying to you inwardly. Some people only hear one sound and say it over and over. That's a good start.

When you receive the baptism in the Holy Spirit, there is no need for dramatic emotion, jerking or falling down. It's just like saying, "One, two, three," and you're off, speaking in tongues. What happens? You hear new words on the inside, where the Holy Spirit speaks to your spirit, and you begin to speak them out in faith. It's that simple.

Now that you know all the reasons why the devil doesn't want you to speak in tongues, it's time to receive the baptism in the Holy Spirit. Just pray the following prayer out loud and then step out in faith and begin to speak in your new heavenly language.

Dear Lord Jesus,

I believe that You are the One who baptizes with the Holy Spirit. I ask You to baptize me with the Holy Spirit now. I receive the fullness of Your precious Spirit by faith, and I will now begin to speak with other tongues. In Jesus' mighty name I pray, Amen.

Signed:_____

ENDNOTE

1. Roberts Liardon, *Why the Devil Doesn't Want You to Pray in Tongues* (Laguna Hills, CA: Embassy Publishing, 1999).

Appendix I

DOCTRINES AND TEACHINGS OF THE APOSTOLIC FAITH MISSION

THE following doctrines and teachings were preached and embraced by the Azusa Street Mission and are taken from the newspaper, *The Apostolic Faith*. Each issue listed most of these statements of faith. The statements on the ordinances of God are found in Volume 10.

THE APOSTOLIC FAITH MISSION

Stands for the restoration of the faith once delivered unto the saints: the old time religion of campmeetings, revivals, missions, street and prison work and Christian Unity everywhere.

Repentance—Mark 1:14,15.

Godly Sorrow for Sin, Example—Matthew 9:13; 2 Corinthians 7:9-11; Acts 3:19; Acts 17:30-31.

Confession of Sin—Luke 15:21; Luke 18:13.

Forsaking Sinful Ways—Isaiah 55:7; Jonah 3:8; Proverbs 28:11.

Restitution—Ezekiel 33:15; Luke 19:8.

Faith in Jesus Christ.

First Work

Justification is that act of God's free grace by which we receive remission of sins. Acts 10:42,43; Romans 3:25.

Second Work

Sanctification is the second work of grace and the last work of grace. Sanctification is that act of God's free grace by which He makes us holy. John 17:15-17, "Sanctify them through Thy Truth; Thy Word is truth." 1 Thessalonians 4:3; 1 Thessalonians 5:21; Hebrews 13:12; Hebrews 2:11; Hebrews 12:14.

Sanctification is cleansing to make holy. The disciples were sanctified before the Day of Pentecost. By a careful study of Scripture, you will find it is so now: "Ye are clean through the Word which I have spoken unto you." (John 15:3; 13:10); and Jesus had breathed on them the Holy Spirit (John 20:21,22). You know, that they could not receive the Spirit if they were not clean. Jesus cleansed and got all doubt out of His church before He went back to glory.

The Baptism of the Holy Spirit is a gift of power upon the sanctified life; so when we get it we have the same evidence as the Disciples received on the Day of Pentecost (Acts 2:3,4), in speaking in new tongues. See also Acts 10:45, 46; Acts 19:6; 1 Cor., 14:21. "For I will work a work, in your days which ye will not believe though it be told you" (Hebrews 1:5).

Healing

We must believe that God is able to heal—"I am the Lord that healeth thee." James 5:14; Psalms 103:3; 2 Kings 20:5; Matthew 8:16-37; Mark 16:16-18. "Behold I am the Lord, the God of all flesh; is there anything too hard for Me?" (Jeremiah 22:27).

Too many have confused the grace of sanctification with the enduement of Power, or the Baptism of the Holy Spirit; others have taken "the anointing that abideth" for the Baptism, and failed to reach the glory and power of a true Pentecost.

The Blood of Jesus will never blot out any sin between man and man they can make right; but if we can't make wrongs right the Blood graciously covers (Matthew 5:23-24).

We are not fighting men or churches, but seeking to displace dead forms and creeds and wild fanaticism with living, practical Christianity. "Love, Faith, Unity" are our watchwords, and "Victory through the Atoning Blood" our battle cry. God's promises are true. He said, "Be thou faithful over a few things, and wilt make thee ruler over many." From the little handful of Christians who stood by the Cross when the testing and discouragement came, God has raised a mighty host.

THE ORDINANCES TAUGHT BY OUR LORD
(*THE APOSTOLIC FAITH*, VOL. 10)

We believe in three ordinances in the church, foot washing, and the Lord's supper and water baptism.

Foot Washing (John 13)

Dear loved ones; it is so sweet to think of that wonderful love that our Christ has for His dear people. Oh, beloved, just think of our Almighty Christ. He became a servant, and washed the disciples' feet. This is the first place in the scriptures where we see Jesus using water, a very type of regeneration, washing the disciples' feet. The Word speaks of regeneration as the washing of water. This ordinance is a type of regeneration. Jesus is the Word. "Now ye are clean through the Word which I have spoken unto you." John 15:3.

Jesus washed the disciples' feet, and exhorted them to humility and charity. Bless His holy Name. We read in the Word of God, "Now before the feast of the Passover, when Jesus knew that his hour was come that

He should depart out of this world unto the Father, having loved His own which were in the world, He loved them unto the end (Bless God! Praise His holy name!) Supper ended, the devil having now put into the heart of Judas Iscariot, Simon's son, to betray Him. Jesus knowing that the Father had given all things into His hands, and that He was come from God, and went to God; He riseth from supper and laid aside His garments; and took a towel and girded Himself. After that he poureth water into a basin and began to wash the disciples' feet, and to wipe them with the towel wherewith He was girded." John 13:1-4.

We read where Jesus cometh to Simon Peter and Peter said unto Him, "Lord, dost Thou wash my feet?" Jesus answered and said unto him, "What I do, thou knowest not now, but thou shalt know hereafter." We can see that this was something new to Peter. He was not used to the Master's washing his feet. The Lord Jesus told him he should know hereafter. What Jesus means was that when the blessed Holy Spirit should be poured out after the resurrection and ascension unto heaven, that this blessed Holy Spirit would lead Peter into all the doctrines of Jesus. They would be practiced just as Jesus said in John 16:12; "I have yet many things to say unto you, but ye cannot bear them now. Howbeit when He the Spirit of truth is come He will guide you into all truth, for He shall not speak of Himself, but whatsoever He shall hear that shall He spoke, and He will show you things to come. He shall glorify Me, for He shall receive of Mine and shall show it unto you."

Peter said unto Him, "Thou shalt never wash my feet." Jesus answered, "If I wash thee not, thou hast no part with Me."

Dear beloved, none of us should reject the command of our Lord and Savior, Jesus Christ, or these different ordinances that He has instituted. By what right do we dictate to our blessed Master? He said so tenderly, "If I wash thee not, thou hast no part with Me." This was a rebuke also to any man or any woman that thinks they are independent of the teachings of Jesus. When Peter heard this rebuke, he said to the Lord, "Lord, not my feet only but also my hands and my head." How these disciples loved Jesus after that. Jesus said to him, "He that is washed needeth not save to wash his feet but is clean every whit, and ye are clean but not all."

So after He had washed their feet and had taken His garments and was set down again, He said unto them, "Know ye what I have done unto you? Ye call me Master and Lord and ye say well for so I am. If I then your Lord and Master, have washed your feet, ye ought also to wash one another's feet." Why? Well we only have to read the next verse for ourselves, "For I have given you example."

Dear beloved, we can see this is humility towards each other in real love. While it does mean that, suppose we all practice it literally, for Jesus is our example. He said, "I have given you an example that ye should do as I have done unto you." Some may say that the manner and customs have changed from that day, as we no longer wear sandals, but, dear ones, are our manners and customs going to change the Word of God? "Verily, Verily I say unto you, the servant is not greater than his Lord, neither he that is sent greater than He that sent him. "If ye know these things, happy are ye if ye do them." Now this is to His true believers, because they are worthy. Verse 18 explains just who should not do it. He says, "I speak not of you all, for I know whom I have chosen." Dear beloved, if the Lord has chosen us, He has chosen us to walk in the light, as He is in the light, that we might have fellowship one with another, and the Blood of Jesus Christ His Son cleanseth us from all sin. Amen.

Jesus Himself instituted foot washing in the New Testament, not as in the Old Testament when the priest would wash his own feet at the lever in the temple that represented regeneration, but Jesus Himself washed the disciples' feet and wiped them with the towel. Therefore, dear loved ones we believe that foot washing is one of the ordinances of the church of God. We find that it is a service much blessed of God to our souls. It is for the disciples, not for sinners. In this service the sisters will assemble by themselves apart and wash each other's feet and the brothers will wash the brother's feet. This is also a service of testimony, song and praise. After that comes the Lord's supper.

The Lord's Supper

The Lord Jesus ate the Passover with His disciples; that was Moses' law. It was not finished forever, as He shoved that table aside, and after washing the disciples' feet, instituted the Lord's supper, the Christian Passover, the bread and the wine. The Passover was the very type of Jesus. It had a three-fold meaning; the sprinkled blood for redemption; the body of the lamb eaten for health and healing; and the passing over the Red Sea that was a type of the Blood of Jesus Christ that gives us victory over all the powers of the enemy.

"The Lord Jesus in the same night in which He was betrayed, took bread; and when He had given thanks, He brake it and said, Take, eat, this is My body that is broken for you; this do in remembrance of Me. After the same manner also He took the cup, when He had supped, saying This is the new testament in My Blood; this do ye, as oft as ye drink it, in remembrance of Me. For as oft as ye eat this bread and drink this cup, ye do show the Lord's death until He come" (1 Corinthians 2:23-26). Praise His holy name. We see that this ordinance points us to the coming of the Lord, our great deliverance, as the Passover was the deliverance of the children of Israel from Egypt.

The Passover supper always reminded the Jews of God's great love for them in delivering them out of Egyptian bondage. It was by blood that pointed them to the Lamb of Calvary. The Lord's supper is to us a memorial of the death of our Lord and points us to His coming to catch us away in the glorious liberty of the children of God.

They ate the Passover, the body of the lamb that gave them strength and healing. The body of the lamb stood for healing and health, just as Christ's body is health to us, "for with His stripes ye are healed." We find as we partake of this ordinance, it brings healing to our bodies if we discern the Lord's body by faith (1 Corinthians 29-30). It also teaches us salvation and sanctification through the Blood. Our souls are built up, for we eat His flesh and drink His Blood. The Lord Jesus promised, "Man shall not live by bread alone, but by every word

that proceedeth out of the mouth of God. May Christ's children everywhere live by every word that proceedeth out of the mouth of God.

Water Baptism

We believe in water baptism, because Jesus commanded it after His
resurrection. Mark 16:16. "He that believeth and is baptized shall be
saved." We believe in water by immersion, single. Matthew 3:16, "And
Jesus when He was baptized, went up straightway out of the water"
(Acts 8:38-39). "And He commanded the chariot to stand still; and they
went down into the water, both Philip and the eunuch; and he baptized
him. When they were come up out of the water, the Spirit of the Lord
caught away Philip, that the eunuch saw him no more; and he went on
his way rejoicing."

It sets forth the believer with Christ in death, burial, and resurrection.
Romans 6:3-5, "Know ye not, that so many of us as were baptized into
Jesus Christ were baptized into His death? Therefore, we are buried with
Him by baptism into death: that like as Christ was raised up from the dead
by the glory of the Father, even so we also should walk in newness of life.
First if we have been planted together in the likeness of His death, we shall
be also in the likeness of His resurrection." Galatians 3:27, "For as many of
you as have been baptized into Christ have put on Christ."

Baptism is not a saving ordinance, but it is essential because it is a
command of our Lord. Mark 16:16, and Acts 2. 28 "Repent and be baptized everyone of you in the name of Jesus Christ for the remission of
your sins." It is "Not the putting away of the filth of the flesh, but the
answer of a good conscious toward God" (1 Peter 3:21). It is obedience
to the command of Jesus, following saving faith. We believe every true
believer will practice it.

A disciple who is baptized with the Holy Spirit and fire, in the name
of the Father, Son, and Holy Spirit should administer it. Matthew 28:19-
20, "Go ye therefore and teach all nations, baptizing them in the name
of the Father, and of the Son and of the Holy Spirit; teaching them to
observe all things whatsoever I have commanded you." We find that

they were first to tarry for the promise of the Father that would qualify them. Acts 1:4, "And being assembled together with them, commanded them that they should not depart from Jerusalem, but wait for the promise of the Father."

We believe that we should teach God's people to observe all things whatsoever He has commanded us, practicing every command and living by every word that proceedeth out of the mouth of God. This is a full Gospel.

Bible salvation will take you into heaven but if you do not have Bible salvation, you will have a great deal of trouble around the gate. Your name will not be found.

We are not called by this country to preach the Gospel, but we are called from heaven, and heaven is not bankrupt, neither is God gone out of business. He does not send us out to preach this Gospel and pay our bills. Do business for Christ and He will take care of you.

"God so loved the world that He gave His only begotten Son that whosoever believeth in Him should not perish but have everlasting life." Oh, today if you have the Lord Jesus Christ in your heart, you have everlasting life. This salvation is real; it is not an influence.

Out of His side flowed Blood and water. The Blood represents cleansing and the water the Baptism of the Holy Spirit. The rivers of living water that Jesus promised flowed out of His side. We get all of this by living in Christ.

The Lord has provided the Word as a looking glass for us to see ourselves whether there are any spots on us. The Word is a washer. "Ye are clean through the Word which I (Christ) have spoken unto you."

When you are sanctified, the old Ishmael of your soul is put out of your house. You are free from the old man. Old Ishmael will not pinch little Isaac any more to make him cry. Jesus Christ is enthroned to that house.

Oh, it is so precious to have the Lord Jesus crowned in your heart. How wonderfully and sweetly the Spirit unfolds the scriptures to you.

You receive the Holy Spirit and He unravels everything from Genesis and Revelation. He starts and unfolds and all you do is to follow on.

The Jews were the very fig tree that the Lord planted. He planted it that the scepter might not depart from Judah. Herod was the first foreign king that swayed the scepter over God's people. Right at that time, Christ was born and the government was upon His shoulder. This fulfilled Genesis 49:10.

"Free Love"-ism and everything of that kind is from the pit of hell. It is a dragon to devour those who get out of the Word. However, praise God, He has given to His children to know these spirits. Such spirits will not be allowed, any more than magicians, or soothsayers, or sorcerers were allowed to be among God's children in the early days.

If you have carnality in your heart and do not get it out, you do not know where it will lead you. As soon as you get the light of sanctification, you must seek at once the cleansing Blood or you will lose all your salvation.

We believe in a real salvation that gives you the witness by the Spirit. Calvin taught a salvation that if you said you had it, you did not have it; and if you had it, you did not know it; and if you lost it, you could not get it again. Wesley taught that if you had it, you would know it, and if you lost it, you could get it again. Jesus said, "He that believeth on the Son hath the witness in himself." We teach that if a man is ensnared by the devil, and has not trampled the Blood of Jesus Christ under his feet and counted the Blood wherewith he was sanctified an unholy thing, he can get back to Jesus Christ by restitution and faith and doing his first works over.

If your heart is open to the Blood of Christ, He will save you. All He wants is a repentant heart that has Godly sorrow for sin, and He will wash you. Though your sins are red like crimson, they shall be as wool. Oh, the promises of God are sure and steadfast, and though the heaven and earth pass away, the promises of Jesus will never pass away. As long as there is breath and life in your body, you can look up to Jesus and He will save you, but if there is no repentance in your heart you would have no desire to be saved. Beloved, if there is one particle of desire in your heart to look to God, you have not sinned away your day of grace. They that have sinned away their day of grace, cannot be stirred any more than a chair. No appeal will move them. Christ has a desire to save every man and woman on the face of the earth.

We do not read anything in the Word about writing in unknown languages, so we do not encourage that in our meetings. Let us measure everything by the Word that all fanaticism may be kept out of the work. We have found it questionable whether any real good has come out of such writing.

AUTHOR CONTACT INFORMATION

Roberts Liardon Ministries
P.O. Box 30710
Laguna Hills, CA 92654
Phone: 949-833-3555
Fax: 949-833-9555
Web: www.robertsliardon.org

Visit the following Website to see rare film footage, photographs,
and voice recordings of Smith Wigglesworth, Aimee Semple
McPherson, A.A. Allen, Kathryn Kuhlman, and many more.
www.godsgenerals.org(http://www.godsgenerals.org)

Additional copies of this book and other
book titles from DESTINY IMAGE are
available at your local bookstore.

Call toll free: 1-800-722-6774.

Send a request for a catalog to:

Destiny Image® Publishers, Inc.

P.O. Box 310
Shippensburg, PA 17257-0310

*"Speaking to the Purposes of God for this
Generation and for the Generations to Come."*

**For a complete list of our titles,
visit us at www.destinyimage.com**

www.ingramcontent.com/pod-product-compliance
Lightning Source LLC
Chambersburg PA
CBHW060756100426
42813CB00004B/835